LAW AND LEGALITY IN CHINA

中國的法律與
法律精神

夢達一

LASZLO LADANY

Law and Legality in China

The Testament of a China-watcher

EDITED BY MARIE-LUISE NÄTH
WITH A PREFACE AND CONCLUDING CHAPTER BY
JÜRGEN DOMES AND MARIE-LUISE NÄTH

UNIVERSITY OF HAWAII PRESS
HONOLULU

© 1992 the Procurator in Hong Kong of
the English Assistancy of the Jesuit Order

Preface and 'Future Perspectives' © 1992 Jürgen Domes
and Marie-Luise Näth

Published in North America by
University of Hawaii Press
2840 Kolowalu Street
Honolulu, Hawaii 96822

First published in the United Kingdom by
C. Hurst & Co. (Publishers) Ltd.
38 King Street, London WC2E 8JT

Printed in Hong Kong

Library of Congress Cataloging-in-Publication Data

Ladany, L. (Laszlo)
    Law and legality in China : the testament of a China-watcher/
Laszlo Ladany ; edited by Marie-Luise Näth ; with a preface by
Jürgen Domes.
        p.   cm.
    Includes bibliographical references and index.
    ISBN 0-8248-1473-8
    1. Law—China—History.   2. Justice, Administration of—China—
History.   I. Näth, Marie-Luise.   II. Title.
KNN122.L33   1992
349.51—dc20
[345.1]   92-3466
                                                                 CIP

CONTENTS

PREFACE

by Jürgen Domes

Between April 17 and June 3, 1989, at first tens of thousands of university students but later millions of people from all walks of life among the urban population demonstrated in Peking and eighty-three other cities of the People's Republic of China (hereafter PRC) demanding human rights, freedom and democracy. From May 13 till June 3, they occupied T'ienanmen Square, the symbolic centre of Communist power in China, organised their own autonomous federations and unions, policed major parts of the capital and began spontaneously to develop their own administrative network.

In the early hours of June 4, units of the People's Liberation Army (hereafter PLA) moved in with tanks, armoured personnel carriers and other heavy weapons and massacred an unknown number of mostly unarmed citizens – probably no fewer than 5,000 – and thus suffocated the movement. On June 6, the ruling Chinese Communist Party (hereafter CCP) embarked on a nationwide terror campaign of Stalinist proportions in the course of which at least 20,000 people were arrested and twenty-nine activists executed during June alone.

Not only did these events drastically change the political scene in the PRC, and particularly its social climate, but they also occasioned radical changes in foreign attitudes towards the Chinese Communist regime. Western politicians and diplomats, business people, journalists and, last but not least, scholars have realised that their optimistic assessment of the PRC's reform policies and opening to the outside world during the 1980s was based on false political premises. The 'rape of Peking' in June 1989 has forced them to understand, as the French President François Mitterrand put it, that the current leadership of the PRC has 'no future'. Disappointment and disgust have taken the place of admiration and glorification in the general Western perception of Chinese Communism. The PRC's foreign apologists have dwindled to a few individuals, some of them figures of international prominence.

The faulty analysis and interpretation of politics in the PRC by many Western observers was, from the mid-1960s to the late 1970s, dominated by four major images of the country: first as an *emerging world power*; then, as a *populist microcosm*; later as a *socialist system that worked*; and finally as a *development model*. All were revealed to be misconceptions in 1977, when the official news media of the PRC began to reveal the truth about the country's political and social experience under the leadership of Mao Tse-tung (Mao Zedong). A considerable number of journalists engaged in reporting on China, and sinologists had to change their opinions.

Yet at this moment a fifth image of the PRC began to develop: of *China, the modernising nation turning towards capitalism*. A large number of Western journalists, economists, diplomats, politicians, business people and scholars, particularly in the United States and West Germany, promoted this concept, ignoring the reality and deceiving themselves as well as the general public with misleading reports and blurred analyses based on a blind love of China and on wishful thinking about its future – which are unacceptable as analytical criteria in social science.

Thus it was only to be expected that this most recent image of China should turn out to be a misconception too. The world learned of its error with the rape of Peking on June 4, 1989.

Since then, the descriptions and analyses of the few observers who took a more detached and critical stance have been vindicated, and the admirers of the policies of economic reform and rapprochement with the West implemented by the CCP's ruling élite between 1978 and 1989 will now have to re-orient themselves. The small number of observers of power and politics in the PRC who got it right adhered closely to five ground-rules:

1. Comprehensive analysis of the official Communist Party media provided their basic source-material, but they broadened the base of their data by interviewing refugees from, and Overseas Chinese visitors to, the PRC, and informants other than officials inside China (wherever and whenever this was possible), and by scrutinising information from Hong Kong and Taiwan, which, incidentally, has often proved to be accurate.

2. Official Communist Party sources were used consistently and their contents constantly compared over the years.

3. They not only tested the reliability of official sources and tried to filter out their factual content, but also attempted to decode the political messages which they often contained. They did this by observing rules of textual criticism developed for more than a century and a half.

4. They combined this textual criticism with detailed knowledge of the relevant personnel and an awareness that even ceremonial texts and protocol lists may have political significance.

5. They remembered to distinguish their personal emotions from their rational obligations as scholars.

The most exact and consistently correct observer of the political and social scene in the PRC for almost four decades was Laszlo Ladany, a Jesuit priest, who died, aged seventy-six in Hong Kong on September 23, 1990. In the last issue of the bulletin *China News Analysis* to be written by him (no. 1248, December 1982), he summed up his lifetime's experience of analysing official PRC sources in 'ten commandments' which can serve as a model guide for all who work on contemporary China:

1. Remember that no one living in a free society ever has a full understanding of life in a regimented society.
2. Look at China through Chinese spectacles; if one looks at it through foreign glasses, one is thereby trying to make sense of Chinese events in terms of our own problems.
3. Learn something about other Communist countries.
4. Study the basic tenets of Marxism.
5. Keep in mind that words and terms do not have the same meaning in a Marxist society as they do elsewhere.
6. Keep your common sense: the Chinese may have the particular characterists of Chinese, but they are human beings, and therefore have the normal reactions of human beings.
7. People are not less important than issues; they are probably more so. A group may adopt the programme of those who oppose it in order to retain power.
8. Do not believe that you know all the answers. China poses more questions than it provides answers.
9. Do not lose your sense of humour. A regimented press is too serious to be taken very seriously.
10. Above all, read the small print!

Simone de Beauvoir called him 'a fanatical anti-Communist full of hatred'. After many accusations in the same vein, Han Suyin finally remembered him as her 'Hong Kong Jesuit friend', 'tall and dignified and admirably versed in Chinese', 'owner of uncommon intellect' who spoke 'with eloquence and restraint' and had 'humour, zest and knowledge'.

For the many sycophants and apologists for totalitarian Communist dictatorship in American and West European contemporary China studies, it was hardly permissible to quote him; they tried to ignore him as far as possible. But for all of us who dared to attempt a distanced and sober view of the PRC, he had assumed an unprecedented prestige as a China scholar; indeed he was the doyen of the international community of observers of contemporary Chinese politics.

Over almost forty years of continuous observation of developments on the Chinese mainland, thirty of which were dedicated to the regular publication of *China News Analysis*, Ladany succeeded in submitting, with very few exceptions, an accurate and precise picture of the PRC as well as foreseeing the future course of events, predictions that were right much more often than they were wrong. When looking back, we see that he was the first among the very few observers who, at that time, realised that Mao's Great Leap Forward had resulted in economic chaos and the greatest famine China has suffered in the twentieth century. In January 1967, he suggested that the military leaders in the provinces were the men to watch in the future. And in his last January edition of *China News Analysis* (by custom January editions were devoted to broad issues), entitled '*Déjà vu*', he drew the first comparison between the developing features of Communist collapse and the final years of Kuomintang rule on the Chinese mainland.

What made him so correct in his descriptions and so reliable in his analysis? There are three facts which help us to answer these questions. First, he knew China and the Chinese extraordinarily well; his sovereign command of the Chinese language (he could also speak a number of other languages fluently) gave him access to all available sources including the extremely important interview with recent refugees from the PRC. Secondly, he had a firm and deep understanding of Marxism-Leninism. His Jesuit training in philosophy had developed an ability to divest Communist ideology of its fallacious prophecies and penetrate the haze of doctrine to unveil the realities of totalitarian rule. Thirdly, he had a deep compassion for humanity, for its universal experience of joys, trials and tribulations.

These three elements came together in a unique analytical approach: a method of qualitative content analysis based on rigid and uncompromising textual criticism. He adopted this too when he was preparing the work which follows – his last. It provides basic introductory information on China in general and the PRC in particular, but it also presents an analytically clear and precise discussion of the role of law, and the meaning of legality in a Chinese context. Furthermore, Father Ladany proffers two basic observations which will have to be taken into account by China scholars from now on. The first is that the period of more than four decades, from 1949 to 1991, i.e. the period of Communist rule, has been the most repressive and tyrannical in all Chinese history to date. And the second is that, despite many deficiencies, the nine years from 1928 to 1937, the period in which the Kuomintang ruled on the Chinese mainland before the outbreak of the Sino-Japanese war, were the best the Chinese people have experienced in the twentieth century. These two observations, if accepted, destroy a number of preconceptions held dear by many observers of the Chinese scene for a long time. And if these preconceptions, based on views heavily biased in favour of the Chinese Communist Party, have indeed been destroyed, this will have to be regarded as Father Ladany's final, resounding contribution to contemporary China studies. Such a contribution will most probably still be considered as 'biased' by those who were consistently wrong in their evaluation of the PRC because of their own pro-Communist bias, and by those who look at the realm of collapsing Communist rule from a safe geographical distance. As a German who observed the complete breakdown of Communism in my own country's eastern part as well as in other parts of Central and Eastern Europe, and who is now daily confronted with the enormous damage created by Marxist-Leninist rule, and participating in footing the bill for the repair of that damage, I consider Father Ladany's last work as going straight to the point.

However, quite apart from his fundamental contributions to the understanding of China, Ladany was also a wonderful person. While never propagandising his Christian beliefs in a patronising manner, he lived a Christian life in a way that was convincing for many and decisive for a few. His loss has deprived us of a great scholar and a passionate man. It has also changed Hong Kong and the international community of China specialists.

It is a small consolation as we mourn his departure to know that he lived long enough to see his native Hungary liberated from Communism.

Saarbrücken, February 1991

PUBLISHER'S NOTE

When Laszlo Ladany died, he left behind two uncompleted manuscripts, the first of which basically dealt with the question of how the People's Republic of China is governed, while the second examined the role of law in the PRC. While Ladany had studied law, and held a doctorate in that discipline, his approach in both these works was that of a political observer rather than of a jurist.

The editor, Marie-Luise Näth, decided to focus on the second manuscript and to use the first one to complete the text. This was because in both manuscripts Ladany devoted the greater part to the problem of 'Law and Legality in China' – a crucial issue both in China's political and social reality and in the Western perception of this reality.

The editor organised the chapters and formulated the titles of both the book and the chapters and sub-chapters. But with the exception of two passages in Chapters 5 and 6, which are easily identifiable from a footnote or a different style of writing, the content of the book is Ladany's work.

Since the book is primarily for non-specialists – lay persons interested in China or beginners in the field of contemporary China studies – all Chinese names have been romanised according to the frequency of their former romanisation and not in the Pinyin system which has gained wide currency in Western publications since the late 1970s. However, the Pinyin romanisation of personal names of prominent individuals of modern times is added in brackets where they first occur.

INTRODUCTION

Mao Tse-tung abhorred the notions of law and of a legal system. For him, a legal system meant rigid rules that would dam up the free flow of the revolution. In this he diverged sharply from the rulers of the Soviet Union, which had a legal system of its own. Mao would not have admitted that Soviet law strengthened the Communist system rather than weakening it.

Stalin's Soviet Constitution of 1936 did not introduce legality in the Western sense of the word. The prescription of elections by secret ballot in that Constitution did not mean what it said; the decisions of Party leaders remained the supreme law. Nevertheless the legal system in the Soviet Union did ensure the fiction of stability for many years. Mao, for his part, preferred to have a free hand to steer the body politic as he chose. His political campaigns kept the life of the nation constantly on the boil in both cities and villages throughout the country.

In the Soviet Union the legal system enabled a vicious system to continue. China, on the other hand, was in perpetual movement. In the early 1950s the peasants were given land; a few years later it was taken away from them. The middle-class intellectuals were trusted in the first few years; they were rejected in 1957. The Communist Party was in the saddle in the 1950s; in the 1960s Mao built up the military and the military became the rulers of the country. Purges swept through the whole country. In the 1950s those who spoke evil of the Soviet Union were prosecuted and sent to labour camps; in the 1960s those who spoke well of it joined them in the same camps. Those who opposed Lin Piao (Lin Biao), Mao's successor-designate, went to labour camps in the 1960s right up to Lin Piao's fall in 1971. This process of revamping the whole system even survived Mao's death.

The political and legal instability of the second half of the twentieth century contrasts sharply with the tradition of two millennia that preceded it. The long history of China was punc-

1

tuated by upheavals; but its civilisation outlived all of them, saved always by a stable system of laws that remained fundamentally unchanged.

The history of the legal system in China is not widely known in the West. Western people tend to believe that in earlier centuries China was ruled not by law but only by arbitrary despotism with cruel punishments extending at times to the complete extermination of the clan of a delinquent; that the concept of a division of powers was unknown; and that it lacked an independent judiciary or any of the civilised refinements of Western legal systems.

When Western powers occupied the coastal cities of China after the Opium War of 1839–42, they hurried to gain extra-territorial judicial power. Lawsuits were exempted from Chinese jurisdiction and were judged according to the laws of the occupying powers. Chinese law was dismissed as something barbaric.

It did not occur to these intruders to reflect on the comparative novelty of the legal systems they were introducing. Modern legal institutions were introduced in the West only one or two centuries ago, the separation of criminal law from civil law dates only from the eighteenth century; the old English law knew no distinction between them, and in the old Germanic law inhuman punishments, including the cutting off of hands, were common. Up till the end of the eighteenth century, 'quartering', cutting off the tongue, banishment and other extreme punishments were part of French law. The principle of *nulla poena sine lege* (no punishment without law) was first propounded by Beccaria at the end of the eighteenth century. Calvinist legislation followed an ancient Roman dictum: *princeps legibus solutus* (the ruler is not bound by laws). The modern concepts underlying continental law date from the promulgation of the Napoleonic Code. The twentieth century witnessed the rejection of basic human legality by Nazi Germany and the indiscriminate carpet-bombing of German cities by the Allies.

Our modern legal systems themselves leave much to be desired. Is it right to crowd our prisons with people who have made slips, whose crimes have long been forgiven by God and man, and who do not endanger public safety? Have we found a way of dealing with terrorism? Has international public law reached more than an embryonic stage?

China began to introduce modern Western legal institutions a century after they appeared in the West – a process that suffered a severe setback from Mao's imposition of lawless arbitrary rule in the middle of the twentieth century. Not till the years after Mao's death in 1976 did scholars in China begin to write about ancient Chinese law. In 1984 teachers of law at the best universities formed a committee for the publication of thirty books on Chinese law, two of which were to deal with ancient law. In 1985 a single author, Ch'iao Wei (Qiao Wei), published *T'ang Law Studies*[1] which gives a useful historical background to eighth-century T'ang (Tang) legislation, and analyses T'ang law point by point. It is a valuable book, though marred by Marxist oddities – saying for instance that in China feudalism lasted 2,000 years and that laws were the tools of a feudal ruling class for the oppression of the people. In fact, T'ang law itself takes account of private land and property and their protection. Indeed the free purchase and sale of land had begun even earlier, in the second century BC.

In 1986 some serious Chinese reviews dealt with Chinese legal history. However, few of the articles showed deep knowledge of the subject.

An article in *Chinese Social Sciences*[2] asserted that law in the Chinese past spoke of duty only and that the concept of rights of persons was unknown. It was merely a tool in the hands of the rulers – the prince and his ministers. It was rule by man, not by law, based on the Confucian moral teaching that if the individual has an upright character, the family will be properly regulated and the country and the universe well governed.

Another article in a learned periodical,[3] dealing with traditional Chinese culture, said that ancient China had a legal system

---

[1] *Tang Law Studies* 喬偉著：唐律研究 by Qiao Wei, 1985, Shantung People's Publishing House.
[2] *Chinese Social Sciences* 中國社會科學, no. 4, 1986, reprinted in *Hsin-hua Digest* 新華文摘, no. 9, 1986, p. 16.
[3] *Wen Shi-zhe* 文史哲 (Literature-History-Philosophy), Shantung University, no. 5, 1986, p. 20.

and that there was a tradition of observing the law, but that the system was obscurantist and primitive, extolling the rich and despising the poor, giving absolute power to the head of the family and entitling the state to exterminate whole clans.

These were the views of Chinese scholars who had not specialised in the history of Chinese law. What they said was merely what the Europeans had held when they came into contact with China in the nineteenth century.

1

PRELIMINARY NOTIONS

If you put the question 'What is China?' to an average educated Westerner, what will be the answer? What mental associations does the word 'China' produce? The answer would probably be very different in America and in Europe. North America feels closer to China, separated from it only by the oceans. For a century now many Chinese have lived in North America. In the old days the image of a Chinese was that of a laundryman, but since the Second World War an appreciable number of intelligent Chinese have been educated in North America and many have become renowned professors. The image has changed. The United States, moreover, was involved in China during the Second World War and its government was also deeply involved in its aftermath there. Ever since then it has been debated whether the United States could have prevented the Mao regime from turning to the Soviets. After the Communist take-over in China came the Korean War, the recovery of the old Nationalist Chinese forces on Taiwan and, ten years later, the massive United States military presence in Vietnam. American history and American emotions are closely linked with China.

Europeans feel that China is very far away. They have closer ties with Africa and even with Latin America. The British ruled India for a long time, but anything further to the East was of interest to relatively. For Europeans, apart from politicians, the image of China is the historical one rather than the China of the nineteenth and twentieth centuries. To an educated European China means an ancient civilisation, the Celestial Empire, brilliant painting, incomprehensible 'chinoiserie', Marco Polo and Matteo Ricci, a land of culture and art. Yet, apart from a few sinologists, even educated Europeans have a very incomplete picture. They know China only from second or third hand, and often biased

5

sources. There is an immense wealth of Chinese historical writing and literature, but few of these works have appeared in translation. Thus, European knowledge of China has wide gaps. A German professor of international law, an authority on the subject, once gave a lecture in which he asserted that China had never had any knowledge of law. He had never heard of the legal system in China, with legal codes for every dynasty, a system different from Roman law but no less imposing.

Many know that China invented paper, but not that it began using paper currency under the Sung Dynasty, a millennium ago, or that discussion of the influence of the volume of currency on the value of money and on other economic problems had begun even earlier.

ATTRACTION AND REPULSION

For hundreds of years the image of China has fluctuated between extremes. The first foreigners in China, Jesuit priests who studied the Chinese language and culture and drew the first scientific maps of the country in the service of the Chinese Emperor, described the ancient civilisation of the Chinese, their classical literature and their system of government in sympathetic terms.

They can hardly have expected their reports to exercise much influence on intellectual currents in Europe, yet this happened. Many of the most influential European philosophers studied the Chinese system and admired the Confucianist and Taoist philosophies. The influence of China on Leibniz (1646–1716) is well known. He was impressed by the rational social order of China, the respect for law, the social stability and the moral system. He was followed at the beginning of the eighteenth century by Christian Wolff (1679–1754), who believed that there was no conflict between Chinese moral teaching and Christianity. Jean-Jacques Rousseau (1712–78) was convinced that the Chinese emperors followed the dictates of the will of the people. Voltaire (1694–1778) used the reports of the Jesuits to attack their authors, holding that the emperor of China was comparable to a philosopher-king. Such divergent figures as Samuel Johnson

(1709–84), Goethe (1749–1832) Adam Smith (1723–90), and Malthus (1766–1834) studied China. In the eighteenth century there was a craze for 'chinoiserie' in Europe, for Chinese porcelain, lacquer and landscape gardening.

There was also another trend, that condemned the Chinese system. This began with the Dutch travellers in the seventeenth century, who were sceptical about China and critical of it. Montesquieu (1689–1755) considered the Chinese government system repressive and despotic: it did not accord with his own theory. François Quesney (1694–1774) wrote a book entitled 'The Despotism of China'. Rousseau considered Chinese civilisation over-refined, superficial and degenerate. Hegel (1770–1831) believed that the Chinese had no interest in abstract knowledge, that China was stagnant. The poet Tennyson (1809–1892) summed up this attitude in the well-known line (in *Locksley Hall*) 'Better fifty years of Europe than a cycle of Cathay'.

In the nineteenth century, when the forcible reopening of the ports allowed foreigners to enter China, many of those who wrote about it were ignorant of the Chinese language and culture, and focused on everything that pandered to their sense of Western superiority. Considering the Chinese unscientific, backward and underdeveloped, they saw in China only a depraved society full of base vices. The historian Leopold von Ranke (1795–1886) believed that the Chinese classics were unreliable mythical tales. Others like Ferdinand von Richthofen (1833–1905) saw only a potential source of markets, raw materials and cheap labour. Next came the first murmurs about the China of the future, a menace to the world, the Yellow Peril.

There was no Yellow Peril. China was being utterly humiliated by the competing Western powers, which were displaying their military superiority, carving out coastal regions and setting up Western courts on Chinese territory. To this was added defeat by the Japanese. China was no longer the centre of the world, and its historic pride in the superiority of Chinese institutions and culture had been deeply wounded. However, it was not paralysed by defeat. With startling resilience, it set itself to learn and to act; and began a powerful process of introspection. The leading figure at the beginning of the twentieth century, Liang Ch'i-ch'ao (Liang Qichao, 1873–1929), was torn between bitter condemnation of China's traditional system and deep love of his country. As Joseph R. Levenson wrote in his classic work on Liang: 'Liang is no admirer of the Chinese character forged in the crucible of history. In his frequent, ringing praise of Britain, he means to shame China by comparison; witness his comment that Chinese have none of the English virtues, neither self-respect, common sense, nor the ideal of the "gentleman", who treats others, of whatever status, with politeness and respect.'[1] Yet Liang was proud of being Chinese and believed that China would rise again to sublime heights.

During Liang Ch'i-ch'ao's life time, China went through dramatic changes. Lu Hsün (Lu Xun, 1881–1936), Liang's contemporary, was a man of entirely different temper. An erratic and bitterly sarcastic writer, he started off at the age of forty with brilliant, vitriolic short essays. The first was 'A Madman's Diary'. The Madman read Chinese history extolling virtue and morality, and between the lines found cannibalism throughout history. He was afraid of being eaten by his own family. 'How can a man like myself after 4,000 years of man-eating history – even though I knew nothing about it at first – ever hope to face real men?'[2]

His 'The True Story of Ah Q' (1921), which became a classic, was the story of a simple-minded peasant, humiliated, knocked around, condemned to death by mistake, an angry revolutionary, incapable of defending himself – a symbol of the old China caught up in the whirlwind of modern times.

Hu Shih (Hu Shi, 1891–1962) in 1919 brought John Dewey to China, and under his influence the whole educational system was transformed. Hu Shih himself advocated materialism and Westernisation, arguing against the early Communists, who were also bringing in Westernisation in the form of the German Karl

---

[1] Joseph R. Levenson *Liang Ch'i-ch'ao and the Mind of Modern China* (Cambridge, Mass., 1953), University of California Press, Berkeley and Los Angeles, 1967, p. 140.
[2] Lu Hsün, 'A Madman's Diary' in *The Complete Stories of Lu Xun*, Transl. by Yang Xianyi and Gladys Yang, published in association with Foreign Languages Press, Peking, by Indiana University Press, Bloomington, 1981 (pp. 1–12), p. 12.

Marx (1818–83) and the Russians Lenin (1870–1924) and Stalin (1879–1953).

Liang Shu-ming (Liang Shuming, 1893–1988) dreamt of reform of the Chinese village and of Chinese society. He was to be condemned by Mao in the 1950s, but was again highly respected in the 1980s when he was in his nineties.

There was also Lin Yü-t'ang (Lin Yutang, 1895–1975), whose witty English-language book *My Country and My People* (1935) captured Western readers. 'Every Chinese is a Confucianist when he is successful and a Taoist when he is a failure.'[3] For Lin Yü-t'ang the Chinese are *bon vivants* who are not interested in religion or logic. 'An equally undesirable effect of the Chinese spirit of reasonableness and its consequent hatred of logical extremes has been that the Chinese, as a race, are unable to have any faith in a system. For a system, a machine, is always inhuman, and Chinese hate anything inhuman. The hatred of any mechanistic view of the law and government is so great that it has made government by law impossible in China.'[4] Again: 'The Chinese are the worst fighters because they are an intelligent race, backed and nurtured by Taoistic cynicism and a Confucian emphasis on harmony, as the ideal of life.'[5] 'Samaritan virtue was unknown and practically discouraged. Confucius said of the gentleman: "Wanting to be successful himself, he helps others to be successful" . . . The family with its friends became a walled castle . . . indifferent toward, and fortified against, the world without. In the end the family became a walled castle outside which everything is legitimate loot.'[6]

Lin Yü-t'ang added to the 1939 edition a chapter on the Sino-Japanese War. However, he proved wrong about the Communist threat in China. 'Will Chu Teh and Mao Tse-tung also become Chinese and mellow and subtle, shun extremism and work towards compromise? The answer is that they have already done

[3] Lin Yü-t'ang, *My Country and My People*, John Day in association with Reynal and Hitchcock, New York, 1935, 4th edn, p. 117.
[4] ibid., p. 113.
[5] ibid., p. 59.
[6] ibid., p. 175.

so. Anybody who knows Chu Teh and Mao Tse-tung will call them anything except communist . . . The leftists have abandoned their specifically communist programme of expropriation of landlords, and have taken a stand for democracy, intending to work as a legal party within the democratic framework.'[7]

What would Lin Yü-t'ang have written if he could have foreseen then the devastation that would be wrought by the Mao regime and the Cultural Revolution?

Bertrand Russell (1872–1970) also tried his hand on China, where he lectured in 1920–1. He could not resist the temptation to write up his impressions in a book which he called *The Problem of China* although in fact half of the book deals with Japan. One short chapter of 14½ pages, with the heading 'The Chinese Character', is an apology for Chinese weaknesses. 'New arrivals are struck by the obvious evils: the beggars, the terrible poverty, the prevalence of disease, the anarchy and corruption in politics . . . But, to compensate for these evils, they [the Chinese] have retained, as industrial nations have not, the capacity for civilized enjoyment, for leisure and laughter, for pleasure in sunshine and philosophical discourses.' The Chinese are a peace-loving nation. 'They admit China's military weakness . . . But they do not consider efficiency in homicide the most important quality in a man or a nation.' At the end of this short discourse he lists, reluctantly, the shortcomings of the Chinese: avarice, cowardice and callousness. 'The spectacle of suffering does not of itself rouse any sympathetic pain in the average Chinaman; in fact, he seems to find it mildly agreeable.'[8]

Such witty fantasies of famous writers have certainly made their impression on Western public opinion. But the question they ask — 'What is China and what does being Chinese mean?' — is too serious to be left to light wit and fantasy.

Chinese studies were pursued with the utmost competence in the early twentieth century by well-equipped scholars in the Netherlands, France, Germany and the United States; but their

[7] ibid., p. 394.
[8] Bertrand Russell, *The Problem of China*, George Allen & Unwin, London 1922, 2nd imp. (unchanged) 1966, pp. 200, 202, and 210.

field of study was Chinese history and literature. Few of them attempted to describe the characteristics of China and its people.

A late exception is Lucian W. Pye. His *The Spirit of Chinese Politics*, though dealing primarily with the political nature of China, conveys revealing insight into China's character. When the Russians want to modernise they look at their internal deficiencies – perhaps owing to their Christian heritage, the doctrine of original sin and the practice of confession of sins. They castigate laziness, dishonesty and undisciplined emotionalism. They struggle to change the soul of man. Other nations lost their identity under colonial rule, or have to engage in a painful search to find their national roots. Not so China. The Chinese do not feel that they have to deny what they are. They may fight against 'imperialism' or 'feudalism' and may want to change the system; but their 'Chineseness' is not in doubt.[9]

Emotional, impressionistic descriptions by foreigners of what China is and what the Chinese are have not ceased to make their appearance.

China still generates attraction and repulsion. This oscillation has become particularly noticeable since the 1970s. President Nixon's visit to China and the resumption of diplomatic contact with China was followed in the 1970s by a spate of enthusiastic dithyrambs on all things Chinese: American society was passing through a period of decadence, while the China of Mao Tse-tung was a model of public order, justice, welfare and equality, with all Chinese united in their love of the Chairman. When, after Mao's death Peking itself revealed the darker sides of the Chairman's thirty-year rule, the tone changed radically. China became a primitive, underdeveloped, uncivilised and dirty country.

China is, of course, not the only country to be described in contradictory terms. Appreciation, or criticism, of any country depends largely on the standpoint, philosophy and tastes of the observer. But China is particularly difficult to comprehend. What the China of the twentieth century is and what the twentieth

[9] Lucian W. Pye, *The Spirit of Chinese Politics*, Harvard University Press, Cambridge, Mass., 1968.

century has meant for China, can only be known in the long perspective of Chinese history.

THE COUNTRY AND THE PEOPLE

Chinese historiography is one of the wonders of the world. It began with *Spring and Autumn*, Confucius' compilation of the year-by-year annals of the Kingdom of Lu, Confucius' native state, from 722 to 480 BC. The annals were continued by subsequent authors. The father of topical historiography is Ssu-ma Ch'ien (Sima Qian, 145–85 BC) of the Han Dynasty. His great work, written in the 1st century BC, arranged the material according to subject in 130 chapters containing altogether half a million words. Ssu-ma Ch'ien's father was official historian of the Han Dynasty, and the son had at his disposal a great mass of written records.

Imitating the example of Ssu-ma Ch'ien, court historians of each dynasty wrote up the history of the preceding dynasty. The sum of their work is known as the 'Twenty-four Dynastic History', which fills 3,239 fascicles. The dynastic histories follow, with some variety, a set pattern. They start with the history of the rulers; then they have chapters on religion, astronomy, music, geography, law, the economy, literature and art, and biographies of contemporary personalities. They are mines of information, comparable to modern encyclopaedias. For ease in handling this immense mass of material, from the time of the T'ang Dynasty, the matter contained in the individual dynastic histories has been collected into comprehensive systematic volumes according to subjects. The last such collections were made under the last Dynasty, the Ch'ing (Qing). The court historians were in a privileged position, and their independence in reporting good and evil was respected, within certain limits. Their histories were supplemented by historical books by individual historians independent of the government.

The historical books did not provide name and subject indexes. In the twentieth century this want has been supplied for some books by the Harvard-Yenching Institute. The comprehensive historical books known as the 'Nine T'ung', published in Taiwan in twenty-three volumes, are accompanied by three volumes of indexes. Very few of these historical books have been translated into foreign languages. However, even if they were translated, their sheer bulk would frighten off the non–specialist reader. The Chinese reader, however, is also dismayed by the intimidating mass of historical writings, and also by the unfamiliar antique style and terminology.

Besides the dynastic histories and the comprehensive compilation, the 'Nine T'ung', there are the local records (*fang-chih*), each covering the history of a single county or city or region. In the Ch'ing period all counties were ordered to compile their regional histories every sixty years: 6,000 local histories, in 90,000 fascicles, have been preserved. Some of these date back to the Sung (Song) Dynasty, but the majority are from the last dynasty, the Ch'ing.

So much for the historical records. It is also necessary to know something about the fluctuations of the boundaries of China throughout history. At times China has been large, its rule extending well beyond the Chinese-inhabited areas; at times its borders have shrunk, with large territories being given up; at times China itself has broken into fragments. Under Emperor Wu of the Han Dynasty, 140–86 BC, China ruled in the north parts of what is today Korea and the southern regions of what is now Indo-China, and in the west a strip of land reaching deep into present Sinkiang (Xinjiang). After the fall of the Han Dynasty, China shrank and was partitioned for several centuries. A sixty-year period in the third century AD became the setting for quasi-historical legends which have been celebrated in song in the theatres of China up to the present day and form the substance of the popular novel that every Chinese knows, the *Story of The Three Kingdoms*.

Throughout the hundreds of years of disruption which lasted till the end of the sixth century, China was split between many dynasties. In the north, the fragmentary territories were ruled by the leaders of alien tribes, dignified with the title of dynasties. These would surge into moments of glory and then disappear. The short-lived Sui Dynasty reunited the country in 581 AD, and it was followed thirty years later by the T'ang, one of the most glorious of Chinese dynasties. Once again the empire extended far beyond the Chinese-inhabited areas. In the tenth century, after the fall of the T'ang, China broke up again under what were called the Five Dynasties, and the outer territories were lost. And it again shrunk under the Sung Dynasty, which in its latter period ruled only the southern half of China. Alien races held sway over large parts of the country, and the Chinese Sung were obliged to pay tribute to the foreign-dominated North and West. Yet the Sung in the south presided over the creation of some of the most sophisticated art in all history. At the beginning of the thirteenth century China became part of the Mongol empire, which extended from the Yangtzu to the Danube, and under Mongol rule, which lasted more than a century and a half (1206–1368), it expanded greatly. After the Mongols came the Chinese Ming Dynasty, which lasted 276 years and brought southern Manchuria and part of the present far-western Sinkiang under its sway. In 1616 an alien tribe in the north, the Manchus, taking advantage of the decline of the Ming, set up a dynasty of its own called the Chin; thirty years later it changed its name to Ch'ing (Qing). In 1644, the Manchus occupied Peking, the Ming capital, and gradually expanded their rule over all China. The Manchus, being a non-Chinese race from the border area, collaborated with the Mongols and expanded the territory of China in the north-west.

Thus for two millennia the territorial history of China was a long tale of expansion and contraction. There was no territorial stability.

The people of China came into contact with many other races, many of them living in distant regions and thus under Chinese rule only for short periods. They retained their own identity, as is clear even today to those who visit the Turkic races in the vast territories of Sinkiang or the Tibetans in Tibet. They remained aloof, with their religions and cultures unchanged. Things were different with the Turkic tribes closer to the interior of China. These lived in a love-hate relationship with the Chinese. Many of them settled in Chinese territories in the north and north-west, and for periods as long as several centuries, the Chinese in the whole of northern China passed under their rule. These alien tribes adopted the Chinese system, intermarried with the Chinese and brought in new concepts and new ways of living, even new military methods. This explains the difference in physiognomy, temper and customs between northern and southern Chinese, which is visible even in ordinary daily life, in food, in taste, even in musical instruments.

Throughout the long history of China, upheavals have caused massive migrations of people from one region to another, caused sometimes by natural calamities and at other times by devastating wars that made peaceful cultivation of the land impossible. These migrations explain why villages or regions can be found where the people speak a language quite different from that of their near neighbours, and historians find it difficult to determine whence they came centuries ago. It is commonly believed that the cradle of China was in the regions around the middle course of the Yellow River (Huang-he), or in general what is now northern China. Yet this is the region where the population later mingled most obviously with non-Chinese races. It is thus difficult to say which parts of China are closest to the original Chinese, and where the ancient Chinese features and ways of living have been preserved in greatest purity – in other words, who are the real Chinese.

In recent times some Chinese scholars have questioned the long-held belief that the upper region of the Yellow River was the cradle of Chinese civilisation. Some now say it was in the north-east (Manchuria), others that it was in the south along the Yang-tzu River.

However the question we are asking here is: how big is China? As we have seen, under powerful rulers the borders of the empire expanded north and south and deep into the west, and under weaker regimes many of these large tracts, inhabited by non-Chinese, were lost. Often it is hard to define the historical boundaries of China, for this involves establishing a distinction between China proper and territories which were under the control, however strict or loose, of the emperor, between neigbouring countries under direct rule and mere tributaries, paying yearly homage to Peking.

The Koreans and the people of Indo-China adopted Chinese writing and Chinese culture and had close political relations with Peking, but Japan, which also adopted Chinese writing and culture, was never a tributary of Peking. Modern Chinese historians claim that Tibet has been under Chinese rule since the days of the T'ang Dynasty, but other historians deny this, on good grounds. Tibet itself extended its rule to the north and south.

In the nineteenth century the Russian empire took great chunks of territories from China in the north, and at the end of the century Japan occupied Korea and the French occupied Indochina.

Despite all these changes, there is a general conviction among present-day Chinese as to what are the true boundaries of China and which territories are integral parts of China and which are not. The general conviction among Chinese, both on the Chinese mainland and in Taiwan, is that Tibet and Sinkiang belong to China, but that Indo-China, Vietnam, Laos and Cambodia do not; that Taiwan is part of China but Korea is not. The average Chinese has only the vaguest of ideas about the vast territories, reaching up to Lake Baikal, which the Russians carved out of China in the nineteenth century. The status of the present Mongolian Republic is a moot question. In Chinese eyes Outer Mongolia is a part of China. This is the view held by Taiwan and also by the government in Peking, which prints 'Mongolia' on its maps and not 'Mongolian Republic', as was done in the first years of the People's Republic of China. Nevertheless negotiations are carried on officially with the 'Mongolian Republic'.

Uniformity could not be expected throughout the whole of a country as vast as China. Even very small countries like Belgium and Switzerland can consist of divergent parts. In China, as in the Soviet Union and the United States, the variations of climate and physical conditions between north and south create sharply contrasting geopolitical regions. In north-eastern China the temperature in winter falls as low as minus 30–40 degrees C.; in the far south tropical fruits grow. As in India, the northern regions of China, down to the Huai River between the Yang-tzu and the Yellow River, is a wheat-growing area, and the staple food is wheat; in the south, rich in lakes and rivers, paddy rice is an indispensable constituent of every meal. In the north the cities are planned in perfect symmetry, the streets pointing to the cardinal points, east and west, north and south; in the south, mainly because of the rivers, the streets twist and turn. There is a great difference too between the maritime provinces and those which are land-locked. The millions of Chinese now living in South-East Asia migrated from the Chinese coastal regions and not from the interior.

Then there is the difference in language. The coastal regions from Shanghai to Canton speak languages quite different from Mandarin. There are, moreover, innumerable local dialects of Mandarin. Nowadays Mandarin is called '*p'u-t'ung-hua*' (putonghua), ordinary common language. However, this common language is far from common. A student who has learned pure Mandarin in Peking (Beijing) travels a few hundred miles outside the city and finds the tones, so important in the Chinese language, entirely different. This traveller will hardly be able to understand what people are saying in the streets in the provinces outside Peking. A Chinese visitor from the northern province of Shantung (Shandong), where *p'u-t'ung-hua* is spoken, would find it difficult to follow a conversation in Ssu-ch'uan (Sichuan) in the south-west, where the people also speak *p'u-t'ung-hua*. Even professors teaching in universities do not attempt to speak pure *p'u-t'ung-hua*: they speak their own local dialects of *p'u-t'ung-hua*. It takes weeks for the students to get used to it and to be able to understand their lectures.

There is extraordinary cohesion among people of individual provinces, and even greater cohesion among people from particular districts in a province. This explains why groups of leaders in the Communist Party originate from the same district. Although there are various reasons for the cohesion among people of the same district, what is most important is that they understand what they say to one another. Mao, for instance, spoke a local dialect that was unintelligible to the average Chinese. That was why he never delivered a speech on the radio. When he was in Moscow in 1957, Peking Radio started to broadcast his speech, but after the first few seconds the announcer in Peking took over and read it. This diversity of dialect is one of the reasons why the leadership is divided into factions and cliques.

Life-styles also differ. A northerner finds it hard to get used to the diet in the south, and vice versa. It can be said that there is no such thing as 'Chinese food'; there is only northern food, Shanghai food, Cantonese food, Ssu-ch'uanese food and so on. Someone from Shanghai regards Peking food as a rough village diet; a Cantonese cannot swallow the spicy food of Ssu-ch'uan.

Uninformed writers about the Communists speak with admiration about the ascetic spirit in Yenan (Yanan), where the leaders lived in caves. But the caves in that region are not like the caves of primitive people. Many people live in the naturally formed caves, which can be made comfortable and which are cool in summer and warm in winter. In the cold plains of northern China village people sleep on a 'k'ang', an elevated brick 'bed' which is heated from outside, and therefore remains warm. A southerner does not even know what the word 'k'ang' means. In the cold winter of the north people rarely take baths and are not very clean. Southerners feel uneasy unless they take a bath every day.

Geographically Shanghai is in central China, but northerners refer to it as the South. Shanghai is cosmopolitan in outlook; for a northerner a Shanghaian is not a genuine Chinese. For a Cantonese, whose language differs greatly from that of the rest of China, all Chinese beyond the borders of Kuangtung (Guangdong) province are aliens.

Not even the Communist discipline could eliminate these strong local feelings. In Mao's later years and to a much greater extent after his death, local patriotism intensified. The local genres of opera, sung in local languages, flourished once again, and memorial halls and statues were set up in honour of famous personalities born in the province or district whose reputations as poets, writers or statesmen had remained alive in the locality.

The government itself had to yield to such local particularism. In every province there is a radio station broadcasting in Mandarin, but in the provinces where Mandarin is little understood, parallel local stations use the local language. The universal use of Mandarin has been prescribed since the early days of the People's

Republic, and from time to time language-study campaigns have been launched, but with a meagre rate of success. Not even the Party leaders have taken the trouble to learn the national language.

All these divergences are found among genuine Chinese. The groups of national minorities hardly belong to the body of the nation. Politically their regions belong to China, but the people are non-Han. The Mongols, the Uighur and Kazaks in Sinkiang, and the Tibetans all have their own ancient literatures and religions which are not part of the historical Chinese tradition. Genghis Khan, ancient Turkish legends and the history of the Dalai Lama are not part of Chinese history and are utterly remote from Confucius and Confucianism, Lao-tzu and Taoism and the tales of the ancient heroes of the Three Kingdoms. The minorities are foreign bodies on the soil of China. They are retained in China either by heavy Han immigration into their territories – today the Mongols form a small minority in Inner Mongolia – or by the intimidating presence of the Chinese military, as in Tibet.

In those distant regions, the non-Han are kept in China by military force. But what keeps the Han Chinese themselves together? What links icy-cold Manchuria with tropical Hainan island? The Chinese are one nation, with one culture and one history. China has known many periods of turbulence, many internecine wars, frequent devastations of whole regions, many reforms and many revolts; but all these were the internal vicissitudes of one nation with one common history. China is not an artificial union of mutually hostile tribes like many new African states. It is not even like present-day Italy, unified not much more than a century ago. The regions of China have no separate historical traditions like those of Scotland or Wales in Great Britain.

China has one historical tradition. The period preceding the Sui and T'ang dynasties in the first half of the first millennium AD, when the north and the north-west were under the rule of Turkic tribes, is long forgotten. Even then, when China was broken up into separate states, the traditional Chinese system was preserved everywhere. This commonly accepted historical background has proved to be a great unifying force. The ancient sages, Confucius and his disciples, the first Emperor Ch'in Shih Huang (Qin Shi Huang), Hsiang Yü (Xiang Yu) and Liu Pang (Liu Bang) fighting for the throne in the second century BC, the poems of Chu Yüan (Chu Yuan) in the 3rd century BC – all these have remained vividly present to the Chinese mind up to the present day. Yet India too has an immemorial cultural history, as has Europe; yet, the possession of historical cultural unity did not form either into a single nation. Why?

One unique factor keeping the nation in China together was, of course, the ideographic writing, which people of various dialects and languages could all read, all using their own pronunciation. To this should be added the early invention of paper and of printing from movable type. Yet writing itself without a common national historical consciousness does not form a nation. The Chinese characters were adopted in Indochina, Korea and Japan, but this did not weld Indochina, Korea and Japan into a single nation with China. The cultural tradition itself was a more potent centripetal force than writing. The Chinese traditions, the ancient stories, the heroes and adventures were known to people who did not know how to write. Writing remained a preserve of the élite and was kept up by the compulsory state examinations which qualified candidates for jobs high and low. The examinations demanded knowledge of the classics written in an elegant, difficult style. Stories from popular novels spread among the illiterate non-élite.

The colloquial style did not obtain rights of citizenship in the realm of Chinese literature till the twentieth century, not indeed till the 1920s, when some newspapers began to publish articles written as people speak. This was a great reform. Mao Tse-tung wanted to take one great step further. He introduced simplified characters, simplified on the principle of phonetics, which meant that a character with a certain sound could take the place of another character which represented a word with the same sound, though with a different meaning. This was diametrically opposed to the traditional system in which meaning comes first and sound is of secondary importance. Mao's ultimate purpose was to reject Chinese traditional writing totally, replacing it by what is called *pinyin* (writing according to sound), written in the Latin alphabet. However, the facts were too strong for him. Many Chinese words can be distinguished only by writing and not by sound. Making sound dominant and writing Chinese in Latin letters proved an impossible task. Mao succeeded only in upsetting the precision of Chinese writing.

For centuries philosophers and their students have been asking what constitutes a state, whether it is the territory, the common language or, as in Switzerland, the common conviction of belonging to one another. There is no single answer to this question, for the situation differs from country to country. In China the most important determining factor seems to be this last, the conviction that Chinese are Chinese, a conviction based on a millennary tradition.

CHINESENESS

What makes a Chinese Chinese, a German German, an American American? This question is easy to ask but hard to answer. Meeting a Chinese, say from Peking, Canton or any other part of this large country, is not like meeting a Japanese or an Indian or a German or an Italian. Not all Europeans have the same temperament, yet there is something which a person from Warsaw and one from Paris have in common. They use the same philosophical concepts, speak in the same terms of religion, enjoy the same music, and read the same literature. In Asia there are greater differences between various nations of the continent. A Chinese has little in common with an Indian and has nothing in common in taste, music, literature or concepts with Muslims, whether from the Philippines or from Pakistan.

Avoidance of manifesting excessive feeling is an old Confucianist tradition. It resembles the old Roman stoicism, and indeed the classic English social virtues. Chinese music has nothing in common with the pathos of an Italian opera, or with sensual Indian songs. The Chinese are not a singing and dancing people. When walking through a village you hear no songs, though youngsters nowadays may sing modern Western tunes. Educated people may quietly chant ancient classical poems, but the number of people who can do this today is small. Local operas are popular, rustic local opera-style rather than the sophisticated Peking Opera, which is not understood now by the young generation. Rarely, however, does the music of the sing-song theatres express violent joy, sorrow or anger.

The same is true of painting. Sublime and exquisite though Chinese masterworks are, it is rare to find in the history of Chinese painting such revolutionary, unorthodox traits as are typical in Japan. Japan has always followed Chinese art faithfully, but using what it has learnt, it frequently expresses the comic, and often the grotesque, with great originality.

Chinese art – tiny human figures in a wide expanse of nature, the Shakespearean empty stages of the sing-song operas, the melancholy of short four-line poems – leaves a lot to the imagination. At the most, it gives discreet indications of deep emotions.

In social life, too, the dominant tone is moderation, quick but not exuberant humour, easy laughter without outbursts of hilarity, humility, self-effacement without servility. This is found high and low on the social scale. Chinese servants and well-trained waiters in restaurants and hotels carry out their duties with courtesy, often accompanied by good humour, but without a trace of the servile attitude of attendants and servants in India. In administration high-handed overbearing bumbledoms may be found in Taiwan and still more on the mainland, but in general a leader, great or small, wishes to seem close to the people. In the obituaries of Communist leaders, even those who killed many without mercy, it is always said that 'he was easily approached by people'. Chinese professors and highly-trained experts, if they care about their manners, are bafflingly self-effacing, unlike their Western brethren who do not hide their knowledge and qualifications. Chinese scholars of international repute will seek to hide rather than display their titles and achievements. Asked whether he likes a certain subject, he may say 'yes', he is interested in it. A considerable time may pass before his interlocutor discovers that the man is a universally recognised authority on the subject he is 'interested in'. Bertrand Russell experienced this when he talked in China with a prominent politician who said he had some interest in politics. Boasting and over-statement are considered bad manners.

Chinese also do not blurt out their thoughts. The straight talk of Westerners impresses a well-educated Chinese as uncouth rudeness, and is received with well-concealed smiles, or with disdain. It is not always necessary to put thoughts into words; ideas and preferences can be conveyed in other ways. Brisk answers are not always desirable; one can wait for the proper opportunity and indicate the reply with proper traditional Chinese suavity. A blunt 'no' is to be avoided. Respect should be shown to the person to whom one is talking, lest he or she 'lose face'.

The Communists did their best to destroy these millennary good manners. They introduced the Stalinist 'criticism and self-criticism', which meant blunt exposure in public of other people's defects as well as one's own. Nothing could have been more alien to normal Chinese manners. When, after the death of Mao, a Party Reform sought to reintroduce 'criticism and self-criticism', it met with quiet but resolute resistance. Chinese manners, terrorised into concealment for three decades, were not dead.

The Chinese expression 'face' is often misunderstood. It is not much different from the French 'honneur'. Losing face is losing honneur and self-respect. Face in China means above all respect for others. If a school teacher is reprimanded in public by the director of the school, he may pack and leave the school because his honneur, his face, has been destroyed. Yet if he had met the director alone he would have accepted the severest reprimand gratefully. His honneur, his face, would have been respected. This applies not only to teachers but also to young students: a child takes corrections easily, but not if it is administered in public.

This respect for others is also a leading principle in the education of children. Many teachers when marking exercises may correct mistakes but they also underline well-written passages in red. In a well-educated family the children are not trained to obey in military fashion when they are told to do something. From their earliest years the reasons will be explained. This is a suave but effective method. It teaches children to think and to respect their parents not through fear but through love. Much of all this has been lost in recent years.

The Chinese in Taiwan have kept much of the ancient culture and traditions, which the government has been deliberately cultivating. In Hong Kong, where for a hundred years the British colonial regime carefully kept Western and Chinese cultures at a distance from each other, the customs of the Ch'ing Dynasty lived on until around the 1960s, when life became prosperous and highly Americanised and the young generation, fascinated by modernity, lost its cultural roots.

In China, sealed off from Western influence for thirty years, the Chinese cultural tradition was eliminated by Mao's draconian measures. The schools, and at home the parents, did not dare to communicate their own way of thinking to the young. A new generation grew up knowing little of traditional Chinese customs and manners. The educated older generation were saddened at the sight of this cultural chaos, but what could they do?

An old professor of philosophy of Peking University, since 1981 head of the Chinese History Society, wrote that after thirty years of silence Chinese culture was now being freely discussed. When the gates were opened, a flood of ideas surged in. Discussion raged round the merits of ancient Chinese culture and the acceptance of Western cultural trends, some defending wholesale Westernisation, others exalting ancient Confucianist virtues and yet others wanting to blend the two.

This discussion took place among high-level intellectuals. The younger generation had no contact with traditional culture and were eagerly learning what they thought were the latest things in Western culture – Freud and Sartre.

The Communists systematically attacked even traditional Chinese politeness. Chinese who had been brought up under Mao, and particularly those who reached adolescence during the years of the Cultural Revolution, were forbidden to use polite phrases, to say 'thank you', 'please', 'sorry' and so on. In the 1980s, in an effort to deal with widespread juvenile delinquency and roughness of manners, the leadership introduced lessons in politeness and published booklets teaching the youth to use those very expressions.

In 1982, the month of March was designated the month of politeness – with indifferent results. Politeness was practised in March, but when April came it was all over. Yet traditional good manners have been maintained in many middle-class families, and it is not unrealistic to hope that one day they will return to the whole of society.

Chinese visitors to Japan, particularly those from the Mainland, are astounded by the extremely formal manners of the Japanese – not in crowded underground trains, but in the shops, hotels and other public places. A Chinese woman does not bow as many times in her whole life as a Japanese woman does in a single day. Chinese may admire this characteristic but they are unable to imitate it. Their mental texture is different. Japan is still a classic Confucian society faithful to the famous Confucian 'up-up down-down', the formula for respect for the social hierarchical order. All are deferential to the Emperor, even when the Emperor has no political power, wives are deferential to their husbands, children are deferential to their parents, and even students in lower classes in schools are deferrential to the students in higher classes. Such ultra-Confucian rigidity of social behaviour has never existed in the land of Confucius. A teacher in a village was *'hsien-sheng'* *(xiansheng)*, Mister, but Sun Yat-sen, the founder of the Republic, could also be called Sun hsien-sheng. Fundamentally, China has always been a deeply egalitarian society. In traditional China, soldiers counted for little. As the old proverb has it, you don't make nails out of good iron, you don't make soldiers out of good men *(hao t'ieh pu tso ting, hao jen pu tang ping* [hao tie bu zuoding, hao ren bu dangbing]). The Japanese, on the contrary, lived for some seven centuries under military discipline, the ultimate realisation of the Confucianist 'up-up down-down' rule.

A glance at Buddhism – first as it is or was in its original strongholds in India and Sri Lanka, and then as it was transformed in China and Japan — throws light on a typically Chinese characteristic. The representations of the Buddha in India and Sri Lanka are austere, skin-and-bone ascetics who have turned away from material life. Buddhism then travelled to China, and already from the seventh to the tenth century AD, the T'ang figures of the Buddha were opulent and richly dressed, and also meditative, handsome. Chinese Buddhist monasteries were open and friendly places in which you could go where you wished, except into the private quarters of the monks. There was perfect freedom and friendly hospitality. In Japan the statues and the teachings followed the Chinese model, but the spirit is austere and the temples are not particularly hospitable. The Japanese military tradition pervaded the monasteries, and indeed the monasteries were themselves part of the military establishment. It would be hard to find neighbouring countries with a greater contrast between their traditional ways of practising the same religion.

A possible explanation of the divergences may be the influence in China of Taoist philosophy. Taoism is an indigenous Chinese creation, unknown in other Asian countries – although some modern Japanese writers have attempted to prove that Shintoism, with its deep respect for nature, has its source in Chinese Taoism.

Perhaps the most characteristic feature of Chinese life is the imprint of the Taoist spirit. There are few Taoist monasteries and these are hidden away in mountains; but Taoist manners create the atmosphere of Chinese life. Westerners find social intercourse in Japanese society rigid and restrictive, building an impenetrable wall between them and their Japanese counterparts – a wall that even divides the Japanese from each other. A foreigner who leaves Japan and goes to become part of a Chinese society in Taiwan or Hong Kong will find social intercourse there easy and friendly. It will be less so in China proper under Communist discipline.

The Taoist spirit is one of freedom, freedom from rigid rules. It is easygoing and comradely, and as such has served as a beneficial corrective to the strict rules of Confucianism.

Yet this impression of easy camaraderie may be deceptive. Strict discipline does exist in Chinese social life although it may not be visible on the surface. A Chinese acquaintance may call you Johnny and not Mr Brown, but, unlike most Indians, he will tell you nothing about his private life or his family, and will entertain you in a restaurant and not at home. His home remains his private castle. At Chinese dinners foreigners will be told to eat as they like, that there are no rules, no table etiquette. It may take them some time to discover that there are many unwritten rules at the Chinese table, rules about when you should start eating, how much you should take from each dish, when you have to raise your glass, and so on.

One characteristic feature in Chinese life is an unobtrusive self-restraint, one may say a historical self-restraint, which remains impassive under a difficult regime either in the home or in the state. Yet a breaking-point will come. The slowly boiling pot explodes. This is true in the individual's private life; it is also true of the life of the state. There have been several explosions in the course of Chinese history, beginning with the First Emperor in the second century BC, who, in the traditional Chinese phrase, 'burnt the books and buried the scholars'. At the end of the Western Han, in 18 AD, suppressed feelings erupted in what is called the Red Eyebrow Rebellion, when the rebels had their eyebrows painted red. In 184 AD, towards the end of the Eastern Han period, there came the Yellow Scarf Uprising.

Several times the old capital, Ch'ang-an, the present Hsian (Xian), a city of incomparable splendour under the T'ang Dynasty, has been razed to the ground with the consequent destruction of all its treasures. In the periods of territorial division there were struggles between the dynasties. In the middle of the nineteenth century the Taiping Rebellion destroyed one ancient monument after another, among them the Imperial Palace at Nanking. In 1900 there was the Boxer Rebellion. In 1927 the revolutionary forces of the Republic in the Northern Expedition destroyed temples and other religious buildings in the North Chinese plains.

There are hardly any ancient buildings in China today. Even the Imperial Palace in Peking has a history of only 500 years. The most ancient Buddhist temple in the Chinese style is at Nara in Japan. Japan and Western Europe have both suffered great tumult, but ancient monuments survived in both. Why have there been these vandalising episodes in the history of this most tolerant and enduringly patient of peoples? An immeasurable wealth of artistic glory has vanished. What remained were bronzes and texts engraved on stone – and the treasures underground in imperial and other graves. Chinese religious belief forbade the disturbance of the resting-places of the dead. Only under the Communist regime have they been dug up.

Chinese can suppress their feelings, whether of love or hatred, for long periods; but they have long memories. Grandchildren express their gratitude to those who helped their grandparents. Similarly, people take revenge for what was done to their family generations ago.

In the political field too, this form of outburst after a delay has been particularly clear in the twentieth century. Even under the Communist regime a change in the system matures underground for ten years. Then suddenly the change actually occurs.

Perhaps the latent Taoist spirit of rebellion explains the violent jerks in Chinese history. This spirit is more than the philosophical teachings of Lao-tzu (Laozi) and Chuang-tzu (Zhuangzi). It is an expression of ancient animistic religious beliefs, joined later to Buddhist mythology. When the Chinese border with Hong Kong was closed in the Mao period, groups of youngsters used to flee, walking over hills at night and swimming across the shark-infested sea to Hong Kong. They had no knowledge of religion and had been taught only Maoism. During this dangerous journey, they instinctively knelt down and prostrated themselves in front of unusual rock formations or trees, imploring the spirits to be propitious to them in their undertaking. The Communists are well aware of these deep religious feelings, which they describe as 'superstitions'. They tolerate the existence of organised religious bodies, Buddhist, Christian or Muslim, because they can be kept under surveillance. However, they persecute 'super-stitions', those amorphous but omni-present deeper feelings of the people which express an inner force and deep-rooted beliefs in a primitive way. The Communists know that this is a latent smouldering social force which any breeze may fan into a devastating fire, as happened in the T'ai-p'ing (Taiping) Rebellion.

Are the Chinese a religiously-minded people? Many people would answer bluntly: no, that they live in an ethics-based world. Compared to Indians, who live with a colourful world-disregarding pantheon, or to the life-detached Japanese who cultivate death and can throw away their lives in easy sacrifice, the Chinese do not seem religiously-minded. Mao Tse-tung spoke of death jokingly, saying that he was going to see Marx, although he was in no hurry to meet the Master. Are the Chinese then a this-worldly materially-oriented people? This is denied by some Chinese scholars, who will remind us that Buddhism penetrated into the whole texture of Chinese life, its philosophy, its art and even its daily language, and that in all ages people have retired into the solitary life of the Taoist temple, that Christian faith has stood up to bloody persecutions, and above all that popular belief and the practice of ancient rites are not dead. In 1986 an article in a learned journal criticised some Westerners like Rousseau and some Chinese scholars like Liang Shu-ming, who had said that China was a country with no religion. 'Their notion of "religion" was too narrow. If we consider religion as faith and worship, a system of forces surpassing ordinary human life, and take account of the variety of religions among the nations, we must admit not only that religions have existed through Chinese history, but that China is a country of many religions . . . Ignoring the religious history of China one cannot understand the political economic and cultural life of China.'

Taoism, the most typical Chinese religion, and the Taoist mentality have created an individualistic society. The traditional Chinese society has no in-built defence against dictatorial central power, no cohesive intermediate infrastructure between individual families and the state. There were, and are, family clans, but there are no cohesive social or geographical groupings occupying that intermediate position. In the nineteenth century Tseng Kuo-fan (Zeng Guofan) was able to raise an army against the Boxers in Hunan, and Li Hung-chang (Li Hongzhang) an army in Anhui, each acting in his own province. These, however, were temporary reactions to special circumstances. Throughout history the rulers of the provinces have been named by the central authorities. There were no professional guilds which formed cohesive forces and structured society, no self-governing city units as in medieval Europe. There were no balancing forces that could assert their own opinions in face of the central power. China could be kept together only by a powerful central organisation, by the ruler, the Emperor who had the Mandate of Heaven to rule the country. He ruled well if he was the right man and badly if he was not. China might break into pieces in separatė kingdoms, but each local ruler would assume the title of Emperor in his part of the country. There was never an organic social infrastructure capable of asserting its own views.

The result of this is that, for good or for ill, the millions of Chinese families can be kept together only by discipline exerted from the central authorities. Mao Tse-tung was perhaps right when he revised one of his early writings in which he had spoken of the possibility of a federal government in China. It is hard to imagine China becoming a union of separate legislatures and governments on the model of Germany or the United States. But this poses an important question about the future of China.

ABYSS

The above may be a fair description of China and the Chinese throughout history. But is it a fair description of what Mainland China and the Chinese on the Mainland are today? Since the middle of the nineteenth century, China has been encountering a world—the Western world—that has proved more powerful and in many ways more advanced than itself. This fact has inflicted a cultural shock from which China is still suffering and has not yet recovered. One after another, the cession of coastal cities to European powers, the humiliating treaties, the military defeat by Japan in 1895, and then in the twentieth century the revolt against Manchu rule, the internal dissension in the first years of the Republic, the Japanese invasion in 1937, and the introduction of the Stalinist system twelve years later, shook the whole edifice of China. Nevertheless, deep in their hearts the Chinese have remained as they were before. The traditional Confucianist and Taoist inner fibres of the Chinese soul were still alive and still strong.

The real break came with the thirty years of the Maoist regime. A reign of fear changed the interior structure of the growing generation. A vacuum was created. The traditional morality, traditional customs and conventional signals used by people to communicate with each other all vanished. This change culminated during the Cultural Revolution and the ensuing years, a ten-year period during which there was hardly any schooling and education, and a generation grew up like wild plants in the jungle.

Outwardly the young generation behave much as young people behave everywhere in the world. But closer scrutiny reveals large blanks in their thoughts and emotions. An abyss separates them from all former generations. This is not the natural revolt of a new generation against the old; it is an emptiness that is not even capable of suggesting what they should revolt against.

Under the Maoist terror, teachers in the schools and parents at home did not dare to talk freely to children. They did not teach the traditional external courtesy, which was totally opposed to Maoist rules. The closely-woven web of traditional culture was not transmitted to the younger generation, who became strangers in their own land. There are gaping holes in their emotional lives. They do not respond with the old feeling to the traditional stories from Chinese history that moved former generations to tears or to laughter. They are unable to appreciate the traditional Chinese theatre that transmitted from one generation to the next the old Chinese stories which carried with them a world outlook, good or bad. The young generation grew up learning only the Maoist dogmas – in which they did not believe – and remained ignorant of what China used to be and what the Chinese were like.

They could hardly have described what they were missing. They were deprived of the whole traditional culture, not as it is learned from books but as it was formerly sucked in with their mothers' milk and breathed in with the air. Anyone who comes close to this younger generation notices that something essential, and something too that is essentially Chinese, is absent. This is a generation that grew up without fundamental norms of behaviour, without value judgements, without knowing what it is to be Chinese. The better among them have a bewildered consciousness of having missed something, and strive to make up for their loss by avidly reading all that they were not allowed to read in their earlier days. Yet such reading does not supply what is absorbed more or less instinctively in childhood.

This generation has now reached middle age. The next generation – the generation of the 'only child' – is cherished, but what are these children learning from their parents, who themselves grew up in a cultural vacuum? What will the mainland Chinese be in twenty or thirty years?

The young generation in Taiwan, at the same time as being fully adjusted to modern life, still remains Chinese in tastes, manners and cultural tradition, but the new generation in China proper will not be the same. Will wild instincts, unrestrained by traditional moral standards, burst out into blind chaos? Or will a genuinely new China emerge, absorbing world culture and becoming part of it, and retaining only tenuous links with the old China?

2

CHINA'S ANCIENT LEGAL SYSTEM
AND ITS END

TWO SYSTEMS

Just as traditional Chinese culture and Western culture are utterly different, so traditional Chinese law and modern Western law are also utterly different. But China – as we shall see below – was not a legal vacuum and many characteristics of modern Western legal life are to be found in China from early times and were codified with ever greater clarity through the centuries.

The Chinese and European legal systems are different in basic structure. The *praetor* in classical Roman law adjudicated the complaints of individuals. Law, one can say, came from below. In China it came from above. The Chinese legal system defined the duties and obligations of individuals, and this in turn indirectly protected the rights of the individuals. It protected their lives against murder or homicide – which were clearly distinguished – and their private property against violation; the orderliness of family life was preserved. It is far from the truth to say that in ancient Chinese law there was no 'civil law', but the starting points in China and in the West were different. The Western system takes as its starting-point the rights claimed by the individual. The Chinese system begins with the state as the guardian of rights and the punisher of transgressors. In Europe an age of absolutism followed the breakdown of the medieval synthesis. In China, at about the same time, the absolute rule of emperors led to abuses at court and, through lack of control, in local mandarinates. This, however, did not arise from intrinsic defects in the system. From the earliest times, the Chinese legal codes prescribed that officials who transgressed the bounds of their authority in judging legal cases, or were negligent in the investigation of cases, should be punished.

A common feature in China and the West was the problem

of the relation between law and morality. The Justinian codification of Roman law in the sixth century, which became the foundation of all subsequent European legislation, was deeply influenced by Christian concepts of justice and equity. It was the legislation of a Christian Roman empire. From this evolved in the Middle Ages the explicit concept of equity – a moral concept – in English law.

The conflict between morality and law began in Europe with the end of the Middle Ages, with their consensus on fundamental Christian principles of morality and justice. In the Middle Ages 'natural law' meant basic general principles only; the application of these principles to contingent realities was formulated by the legislation of the day. The philosophers of the Enlightment constructed their own systems of eternal natural law, but these 'natural laws' were fictitious intellectual exercises, which changed as the political mood changed. This compromised the concept of natural law itself. Natural law fell into disrepute, and jurists dealing with the philosophy of law were, and still are, divided into those who speak of natural law as the firm foundation of legal life and those who believe that positive law alone is law in the proper sense of the word, and that moral principles are outside the realm of law. For these, the ultimate source of law is the legislation of the state. Law is the will of the state. In the twentieth century, in reaction against the arbitrary regime of Hitler and the Nazis, the concept of natural law has reappeared, but the dispute with the positivists still continues.

In China the dispute between those who hold that the state should be ruled by Confucianist moral principles and those who reject that view goes back to the Warrior Period, from the fourth to the second century BC. Some statesmen of the small independent kingdoms in the north of China opposed the teaching of Confucius, the rule of ethical principles, and emphasised the role of promulgated written laws, requiring clear-cut and severe criminal sanctions.

The First Emperor, Ch'in Shih Huang, who conquered the surrounding kingdoms and unified China, adopted the 'Legist' doctrine, condemning the teachings of Confucius and ruling with merciless vigour. But his dynasty did not last beyond the reign of his son, and lasted only a few years. The Han Dynasty, whose rule began in 206 BC and lasted for four centuries, reversed this trend. From then on, the Confucianist doctrine – ethics guiding law – dominated the political scene. The Legists' demand for precise written law was, however, retained.

SOURCES AND SCOPE

In the course of the following two millennia Chinese law went through many transformations. Two characteristics, one Legist and the other Confucian, became blended: the tradition of promulgating dynastic codes and a steady adherence to a set of underlying principles based on the Confucianist world outlook.

Every dynasty, to authenticate fully that it had become established, had to promulgate a clearly formulated legal code, which the local officials were then obliged to implement. With time the dynasty could perfect, change or supplement its code. This ensured a progressive transformation of the system.

The origin of Chinese law dates back to a time many centuries before the beginning of the Christian era, and is to be found in the historical books compiled by Confucius in the fifth century BC. The axioms laid down in these classics were cited as valid basic legal principles for thousands of years, up to the early years of the twentieth century.

Reconstituting the legal system in each dynasty is no easy task. Almost every dynastic history had a special chapter on law, headed *Hsing Fa Chih* (Xingfa Zhi), literally 'Records of Punishments', but, as already indicated, the scope of the ancient *Hsing Fa Chih* had a much wider scope than sanctions. They comprehended the whole sphere of law, including the protection of life and private property. These chapters in the dynastic histories describe the laws of the time in some detail, but they do not reproduce the complete texts of the dynastic codes. Chinese students of legal history have to devote great care to the study of other chapters of the dynastic histories – chapters on the history of the emperors and their courts, on the organisation of administration and of officials and even on the economy of the period. Contemporary monographs must also be used as source material.

Few complete texts of dynastic codes have been preserved. The most illuminating of these are the several legal codes published under the T'ang Dynasty (618–906 AD). Among these the principle code is the *T'ang-lu Su-yi* (T'ang Law and Commentary), a masterpiece of legislation. It is brief and clear, written in common easily understandable language. The earlier Han code consisted of 4,900 articles, containing 7.7 million words, the T'ang Code had 620 articles, containing 136,000 words. This technical mastery in legislation remained the model for later dynasties for a whole millennium, and was imitated in Japan and other neighbouring countries which adopted China's legal system along with its culture.

There was no concept of an independent judiciary. The local mandarins acted as judges. But at the top, among the highest ministries, there was a special board, called *T'ing-wei* (Tingwei) or *Ta-li-ssu* (Dalisi), which supervised judicial cases and acted as the highest court of appeal.[1] According to ancient conviction, unjust government and unjust court sentences could provoke the displeasure of Heaven and thus be the cause of natural disaster.[2]

CONTENTS

The severity of the law was extreme. The *Wu-hsing* (Wuxing), Five Punishments, go back to the earliest times. They include a wide variety of corporal punishments – the cutting off of a foot or of the nose, castration, branding of the face, bastinado, flogging to death, exposure in public places.

With time some mitigation was introduced. The chapter on law in the History of the Han written by P'an Ku (Pan Gu) in

---

[1] *Li-tai chih-kuan piao* 歷代職官表 (Table of Officials through History), compiled by Huang Pen-chi 黃本驥 of the Ch'ing Dynasty, reprinted 1965 (only 2,500 copies printed).

[2] At the end of the sixteenth century a minister submitted a memorandum to the Ming emperor saying that unjust sentences 'must have been the cause of untimely rain and snow and the frequent occurrence of disaster'. Quoted in Albert Chan, *The Glory and Fall of the Ming Dynasty*, Univ. of Oklahoma Press, Norman, 1982, p. 36.

the days of the Eastern Han Dynasty (25–220 AD) describes how Emperor Wen (179–140 BC) abolished bodily mutilation, forbade flogging to death and reduced the severity of all flogging, defining the number of strokes and even the length and thickness of the stick. One severe punishment was exile, which took various forms: a criminal, after corporal punishment, could be sent to the border regions at a shorter or greater distance from the interior of China for a number of years.

One savage feature of ancient law was the extermination of the whole clan. This 'clan punishment', *tsu-hsing* (zuxing), was an ancient sanction for treason. It is recorded in the time of the First Emperor in the second century BC, and was retained by all the dynasties that followed. The chief perpetrator of an act of treason was first mutilated and tortured; then his head was cut off and exposed in a public place. His parents and children were strangled. A few hundred years later, this was mitigated to some extent; women were not executed and children under the age of thirteen years were spared. Under the T'ang Dynasty children younger than sixteen years old were exempt. Under the Ming Dynasty hundreds of members of a single clan were reported to have been executed.[3] This cruel punishment was designed to prevent revolt and, in cases of treason, to preclude revenge by the family clan. Extermination of the clan for treason was instituted, not for the common people but for higher officials who had revolted or were under suspicion of revolting against the Emperor. Obviously this was opposed to the general principle that criminal punishment was meant for the common people and not for the upper classes.

The procedure in criminal cases was exceedingly harsh. Throughout the ages the interrogation of the accused was carried out under torture. This could take many forms, from withdrawal of food and drink to the most excruciating physical torments resulting in death. In the early years of the Sung Dynasty an attempt was made to suppress interrogation under torture, but towards the end of the dynasty the practice returned. Under the Mongol Yüan Dynasty, Mongols, unless accused of murder, were

[3] Shen Chia-pen, *Li-tai hsing-fa k'ao* 沈家本撰：歷代刑法考 (Study of History of Chinese Law), 4 vols, reprinted Peking, 1985, vol. I, p. 80.

exempt from torture. The systematic use of torture continued till the end of the last dynasty.[4]

Paradoxically, along with the cruelty of trials, care for prisoners was prescribed. Under the T'ang law, the accused had to be provided with food, clothing and medicine. If the accused asked for the removal of the cangue, a sort of pillory, and the judge refused, the latter would be condemned to sixty strokes of the cane. If the accused died, the judge was condemned to imprisonment for a year. Subsequent dynasties had similar rules.[5]

There was slavery in China, but it was of quite different kind from that practised in the Roman Empire and in the slave markets of Africa and America. Couling's *Encyclopaedia Sinica* (1917) was correct in stating that 'there are no slave markets and no openly violent treatment of slaves'. Among slaves, it said, there are people who have been sold for debt. This has been the fate of sons, daughters, even concubines; the poverty of the common people is the chief cause. In times of famine, it went on, large numbers of children are sold, partly to save their lives, partly because the price received may keep the rest of the family alive. Many children are kidnapped to be sold as slaves. Girl slaves are sold as domestic servants, but they are not sold a second time, and at their masters' death they share equally in the inheritance.[6] In this Couling was correct.

The most learned of Chinese scholars, Shen Chia-pen (Shen Jiaben) of the late Ch'ing Dynasty, states in his monumental study of the history of Chinese Law that there was no 'buying or selling' of slaves in ancient China. He found references to slaves in the history of the Han Dynasty.

Slaves were treated as items of wealth in the legal codes throughout Chinese history. At the beginning of the twentieth century Empress Tz'u Hsi (Ci Xi) sent slaves to her friends as birthday presents.

---

[4] In Europe torture at trial was abolished in the eighteenth century: in Scotland 1708, in Austria 1776, in France 1785. It was widely practised in the middle of the twentieth century in the Soviet Union and East European countries.
[5] Ch'en Ku-yüan 陳顧遠 , *History of the Chinese Legal System*, Commercial Press, Shanghai, 1934; T'aipei edn 1959, pp. 251–2.
[6] Samuel Couling, *The Encyclopaedia Sinica*, Shanghai, 1917.

Han historical records speak of the protection of slaves. A master who killed an innocent slave was executed publicly, for 'on this earth people are the most precious', but under the T'ang a master who killed an innocent slave was punished by imprisonment for only a year. References to the liberation (Roman Law called it emancipation) of slaves are found throughout the historical books. One passage from the Han period recommended that women slaves who wanted to return to their parents should be allowed to do so.[7] The owner of a maiden slave was obliged to marry her off, and if he failed to do so, he was condemned to eighty strokes of the cane.[8]

The system of slavery, with its pedantic, detailed regulations, persisted till the end of the imperial period, that is, till early in the twentieth century. Thus it lasted more than forty years longer in China than in the United States, where it was abolished by the 13th Amendment in 1866.

Slavery in China and in the West had only the name in common. Slaves in China were comparable rather to the serfs of the feudal period of the Middle Ages. Dynastic codes defined the status of slaves exactly. A slave was bound to his master, but he was a member of the master's household.

The Chinese legal system, despite its severity, was a highly refined system, with in-built restraint and moderation. Legal terms and concepts which are parts of modern Western legislation today are found in ancient Chinese law. Negligence, recidivism and cumulative crimes were all recognised parts of the system even in the earliest centuries.[9] The history of the Han the *Han Shu* written by P'an Ku in the first century AD, prescribed to judges minute investigation of the accused. His words, the way he breathed, the look in his eyes, his whole countenance, his personal circumstances, his social status, his abilities, his usefulness to society – all had to be carefully examined. The judge had to inform his superiors and inform the people. He had to see whether a crime

---

[7] Shan Chia-pan, op. cit. (see p. 37, n. 3), pp. 385–404.

[8] Pierre Huang, *Le mariage chinois*, Shanghai, 1915, p. 226.

[9] Yang Hung-lieh, *Chung-kuo fa-lü fa-ta shih* 楊鴻烈著：中國法律發達史 (History of Development of Chinese Law, Commercial Press, Shanghai 1930, pp. 38–9.

had been committed through ignorance, negligence or forget-
fulness. Children under the age of seven or eight and adults over
the age of eighty could not be punished. When an official could
not decide a case he had to refer it to higher officials, and in the
last instance to the Emperor. These directives go back to the early
Chou (Zhou) Dynasty and became permanent features of subsequent legal codes.[10]

An axiom from the *Li Chi* (Li Ji), an ancient book compiled
by Confucius, is often quoted: 'Criminal punishment is not
applied to the Tai-fu'. *Tai-fu* (daifu) is a general designation for
officials and members of the educated classes. The educated classes
were expected to understand and to follow the Confucianist moral
principles of behaviour. The axiom, however, did not mean that
the higher classes were exempt from punishment. It meant that
they were to be treated less severely than the common people.
Close relatives of the Emperor and of his wife were exempt from
prosecution – as heads of state are exempt today, and as members
of parliament are protected with immunity.

Exemption from the severity of law is found in this century's
Communist regime in a different way. A Party member cannot
be prosecuted so long as he is in the Party. Only after he has been
expelled from the Party can the 'weapon of the law' be applied
to him. Thus there are millions of individuals, many of them
illiterate and far from being educated, who enjoy immunity.

Ancient China had another way too of tempering the severity
of the law. Sanctions were mitigated for Eight Categories of
people, the *Pa Yi* (Ba Yi). These eight categories, as defined in
the code of the T'ang Dynasty, were not restricted to the rich and
the powerful aristocracy. They were:

1. those close to the Emperor;
2. those known to be wise men;
3. men of unusual capacity;
4. men of special merits;
5. officials in the three highest grades of government;

[10] Han Shu 漢書 in *The 24 Dynastic Histories*, Zhonghua Bookstore, Peking, 1959,
1975, 7th edn.

6. men known to be diligent;
7. military men in dangerous posts; and
8. guests of the government.

Even nowadays these categories might receive special consideration from courts anywhere in the world. Membership of the Pa Yi did not, as is sometimes alleged, imply exemption from legal sanctions.

From early days China had an appeal system. For a millennium, from the Han Dynasty onwards, there was a three-grade or four-grade system. In private affairs the process would start in the village, where an attempt was made at reconciliation. If this failed, the case could be brought to the *hsien* (*xian*), the county, and from there to the *chou* (zhou), or in criminal cases up to the T'ing-wei in the Imperial Court. From the time of the T'ang Dynasty, private cases were dealt with by the village. An appeal could be made to the county, and from there to the *chou*. Criminal cases were judged by the county, with appeal to the *chou* and from there to the central government, the *Ta-li-ssu*, the highest judicial authority. The names of the administrative divisions changed from dynasty to dynasty, but the basic structure of this appeal system did not change.

In practice, appeals had limits. In local and regional administration, there was no distinction between the administrative and judicial authorities. The plaintiffs were therefore afraid to appeal against a judgment. Also, sanctions were imposed on those who appealed in trivial cases.

One way of seeking a reduction of the sanction or the dismissal of the case was self-denunciation (*Tzu-shou*; zishou), which was part of the traditional Chinese system. When a criminal gave himself up voluntarily, his punishment was reduced or he might be exempted from prosecution altogether. This, in view of the severity of the interrogations and of the sanctions, was an important corrective of the system. Similarly, under the old Chinese law, the denunciation of one's companions in crime secured lenient treatment.

Amnesty was also an ancient institution. In certain periods it was granted once a year; in other periods, once every three years. It was also granted on special occasions, on the accession of the Emperor, at the birth of his sons and grandsons, at times of natural disaster, when revolts had been successfully suppressed, and when agricultural feasts were celebrated. Amnesty did not apply to cases of treason, but in other cases death sentences were commuted and heavy sentences reduced.

It was the law that death sentences had to be referred to higher authorities for approval. Under the T'ang Dynasty this regulation was so strict that a judge who failed to observe it was sentenced to exile at a distance of 2,000 *li* (about 1,000 km.).[11] From ancient times the executions of criminals condemned to death were carried out in the autumn. The reason for this is to be found in the ancient Confucianist outlook on the world, which saw harmony between nature and human life. Autumn is the season of death.

Ancient Chinese law did not distinguish formally between the civil and the criminal, but in fact considerable parts of the legal codes dealt with the protection of personal rights: of life, of bodily integrity, of personal property.

In the T'ang code, *T'ang-lu Su-yi*, eleven articles dealt with occupation of other people's land. The sanction was sixty strokes for occupying less than one *mou* of land and 100 strokes for occupying more than three *mou*. One article deals with 'the occupation of private land by officials'; fourteen articles deal with stealing; thirty with causing bodily injury. Different sanctions were imposed according to the nature of the injury – whether a hand, a foot, a tooth, an ear or the nose, for example, had suffered injury, whether the injury had broken bones, and so on. If death had resulted without it being intended, the sanction was death by strangling. Where the attacker had a sword and death had resulted, the article referred to the article on murder. The sanctions would then vary according to the injurer's relationship to the person injured – husband, wife or concubine, brother, sister, parent, grandparent, and so on. Robbery was dealt with separately

[11] Ch'en Ku-yüan, op. cit. (see p. 38, n. 5), p. 308.

from stealing. Distinctions were drawn, for example, between stealing followed by violence and violence followed by stealing, and between robbery causing physical injury and robbery causing the burning down of a house. There were many other regulations protecting individuals. A hundred strokes were given to a person who had seen a fire and not reported it, whether the property threatened by the fire was public or private.

The law also dealt with traffic offences. Driving a horse-drawn cart drawn into a crowd was punishable. If such a cart, which was being driven fast, killed someone, the crime was treated as unintentional manslaughter if the vehicle was a public post-cart delivering official documents or if a private cart was on an urgent journey seeking help for the sick or some such errand.[12]

SUMMARY

The above short sketch may not give an adequate description of the history of Chinese law, but it does clarify some points. China has had a tortuous political history. Dynasties were born, flourished, declined and disappeared. For centuries the country was broken up into separate kingdoms, and for centuries it was governed by non-Chinese foreign races. Nevertheless, in its basic elements the legal system remained stable.

In Europe the 'barbarians' who broke up the Roman Empire brought in a new and less civilized legal outlook, moderated only to some extent by humanitarian Christian principles. India had no legal tradition like that of China. Japan and other Asian countries adopted the Chinese system. The stability of the Chinese legal edifice through thousands of years is unique in the history of mankind. Seen through twentieth-century eyes, it may not seem to have been a perfect system; it was severe and often cruel, and it was directed from above. There were emperors who ruled despotically, but none of them attempted to demolish the legal system, and social life continued to be regulated by carefully elaborated legal codes.

---

[12] *T'ang-lu Su-yi* 唐律疏議, 1983, Peking edn.

There were many elements of in-built inequality in society and the state took no care of the sick or the old. There was no social welfare. The state did not interfere with private life. Care of the sick, the old and the unemployed belonged in the domain of the family clan. But order in the family clan was protected – to an excessive degree – by the legal order, and infringements of family or private property, even by public officials, were severely punished. The stability of the legal system ensured the stability of society and guaranteed that people knew their rights and their duties. This stability, however, involved rigidity and incapacity for adaptation to radical change in a radically changing world.

THE END

The world seemed to change radically as mighty shocks succeeded each other – foreign military interventions, the carving off of important enclaves round the coastal cities by foreign powers and, last but not least, the annihilation of the Chinese fleet by the Japanese in 1895, followed ten years later by the victory of a Japanese army over the Russians on Chinese territory in Manchuria.

Emperor Kuang Hsü (Guang Xü) came to the throne as an infant in 1875, but to the end of his life he was overshadowed by the domineering Empress Dowager Tz'u Hsi. In 1898, when still a young man, having come under the influence of enlightened tutors, in particular the statesman K'ang Yu-wei (Kang Youwei), he ordered radical political reforms – the abolition of the ancient examination system, the establishment of a university in Peking, modernisation of the army, and so on. This is known as the Hundred Days Reform, because a hundred days later Tz'u Hsi clapped the Emperor into confinement and arrested and executed several Chinese leaders, among them K'ang Yu-wei's younger brother. K'ang himself fled to Hong Kong.

The spirit of reform was not dead, however. After the Boxer Uprising of 1900, which tore down the telephone lines in North China, destroyed every vestige of Westernisation, and provoked the occupation of Peking by eight foreign powers, the imperial

court itself began the process of modernisation. An imperial edict
in this sense was issued in 1901 by the Empress Dowager. Two
men, Wu T'ing-fang (Wu Tingfang) and Shen Chia-pen, were
entrusted with the task of reforming the Legal Code of the Ch'ing
Dynasty. The sixty-year-old Wu T'ing-fang, member of a Cantonese family of Hsinhui (Xinhui), had been born in Singapore,
and received a Western education in Hong Kong. Having been
called to the English Bar in 1876, he went to China to work for
a great Chinese reformer, Li Hung-chang (Li Hungzhang). He
was one of the few thoroughly Westernised Chinese authorities
on law.[13]

Shen Chia-pen, whom we mentioned when dealing with the
ancient history of Chinese law, was no less an authority; his books
on the history of classic Chinese law are still undisputedly the
prime authorities on this subject.[14] Shen was born in 1840. At
the age of twenty-five he started work in the Peking Board of Law
and for some twenty years was engaged in the study of the history
of Chinese law. At the end of the century he was a magistrate in
a provincial city in North China, and a few years later was in
Peking working on legal reform in the Bureau for the Compilation of the Law, opened in 1904. The Board invited scholars who
were familiar with foreign languages to translate the legislation
of various Western countries. Special emphasis was laid on study
of the Japanese system, and Japanese legal scholars were invited
to China. In 1906 the first Western-style law school was opened
in Peking, and work went ahead rapidly. What was aimed at was
not the creation of a new legal system but a revision, with radical
changes, of the old Ch'ing Dynasty laws. Torture at trials was
to be abolished, and corporal punishment replaced by fines and
imprisonment. A separation of powers between the administration and the judiciary was to be introduced. The Supreme Court,
now independent of the Executive, was to relinquish its old name,
Ta-li-ssu, and be renamed *Ta-li Yüan*. A distinction was to be

[13] Arthur W. Hummel (ed.), *Eminent Chinese of the Ch'ing Period (1644–1912)*, 2 vols,
US Govt Printing Office, Washington DC, 1943–4.
[14] *Works of Ji Yi* (Shen Chia-pen) by Li Guangcan 李光燦著：評「寄簃文存」，Peking,
1985.

drawn between civil and criminal law. Cross – examination and the jury system were to be introduced. In 1907 Shen Chia-pen presented the New Criminal Law, which abolished the traditional *Pa Yi*, the system of milder sanctions for the educated classes. Many of the innovations were copied from Japanese law, which in turn had been influenced by the German Code of 1889. One radical change was the abolition of the distinction between Manchus and Chinese.

The proposed reforms, however, met with sharp opposition, not only from Manchu officials but also from Chinese scholars including Lao Nai-hsüan (Lao Naixuan). Lao was the scholar who was working with the German sinologist Richard Wilhelm on the translation of the Book of Changes, the *I Ching* (Yi Jing). He supported Yüan Shih-k'ai (Yuan Shikai), the ambitious politician who made himself Emperor in January 1916 but held the throne only for three months.

Accordingly, Shen Chia-pen revised the draft code in 1909, and the revision was promulgated in May 1910. In its new form, it still separated criminal from civil laws, but many traditional Confucianist notions had been reinstated. The main changes therefore were the abolition of cruel sanctions, trial under torture and the separation of criminal from civil law. This newly-separated civil law included phrases, picked from the traditional code, dealing with private ownership, land, debts and family law.[15]

Only a year after the promulgation of this reform, the revolution broke out, leading to the abdication of the Manchu Dynasty and the establishment of the Republic. Years of turbulence followed, with cliques of warlords dividing the country between them. Quarrelling politicians, backed by warlords, ran the government in Peking. The revolutionaries, with Sun Yat-sen as their leader, were in the South. Shen Chia-pen died soon after the establishment of the Republic, and no new legal codes were published for twenty-odd years.

[15] Howard L. Boormann and Richard C. Howard (eds), *Biographical Dictionary of Republican China, 1967–71*, 4 vols, Columbia University Press, New York, 1967–71, under 'Shen Chia-pen' and 'Lao Nan-hsuan', and Yang Hung-lieh, op. cit. (see p. 39, n. 9).

The loyalists who were opposed to the suppression of the monarchial system were deeply disturbed by the new events. K'ang Yu-wei, who had narrowly escaped with his life when he attempted to modernise China in 1898, opposed the Republic and worked for the restoration of the monarchy. An infant had inherited the throne in 1906. The baby Emperor's dynastic title was Hsüan T'ung (Xuantong); but China's last Emperor is more widely known by his personal name, P'u Yi (Pu Yi). He abdicated formally in February 1912, but did not leave the Imperial Palace till 1923. In the 1930s he became the nominal Emperor of Manchukuo, then occupied by the Japanese. P'u Yi thus returned to the homeland of his ancestors. He spent years in prison under the Communists and died in 1967.

One of the most remarkable figures of early Republican days was Wang Kuo-wei (Wang Guowei), an outstanding historian. He remained loyal to the deposed Emperor P'u Yi and when Chiang Kai-shek's Southern Army approached Peking in 1924, he killed himself.[16]

Passion is stronger than reason. The revolution of 1911 swept away the painstaking work of Shen Chia-pen and others who had been working for the modernisation of China without revolution. But when the revolution broke out, the texts of a civil code, a code for commerce and a criminal law were ready.[17]

Some legislative effort continued after the establishment of the Republic. The old Chinese tradition of establishing a legal foundation for a new regime was not dead. The towering figure in the legal world was Wang Ch'ung-hui (Wang Chonghui), a lawyer of international reputation who in the 1920s became a member of the World Court. At home he stood above party divisions, filling major political roles first in Peking in the tumultuous post-revolution governments and then, after the establishment of Chiang Kai-shek's Nationalist government, in the new capital, Nanking. In the first years of the Republic he collaborated actively with the legislative efforts of one French and two Japanese lawyers. Drafts of a code of criminal law and a code of civil law,

[16] ibid., under 'Wang Kuo-wei'.
[17] Jean Escarra, *Le Droit Chinois*, Peking, 1936, pp. 108–9.

and rules of procedure of civil and criminal law were drawn up. These drafts remained drafts, but they had considerable influence on the legal life of China in the years when the country was in political turmoil.[18]

Immediately after the revolution, Sun Yat-sen was elected President of the Republic, and in March 1912 a provisional Constitution was promulgated. Soon after this, Sun ceded the presidency to Yüan Shih-k'ai. A new Constitution was published in Peking with increased presidential powers; then, after the fall of Yüan in 1916, Li Yüan-hung (Li Yuanhong), the new president, reinstated the 1912 provisional Constitution. With every change in the fluctuating political life, a new attempt would be made to define the powers of the state until Chiang Kai-shek set up the Nationalist government in Nanking in 1928. His Nationalist Part, the Kuomintang, proclaimed in 1928 the beginning of a period that was called 'political tutelage', during which the nation would be prepared for normal administration. The transition period was to last till 1935.[19]

The 'tutelage', which meant education of the nation in understanding of political institutions, was more realistic than earlier attempts at radical change for which the people, unaccustomed to anything but imperial rule, had been quite unprepared. But did tutelage mean that the Nationalist Party would give up its unique role in 1935?

In the early 1920s Sun Yat-sen, the founder of the Kuomintang, listened to Russian advisers. He reorganised his party on the Soviet model, and on the basis of the Communists having individual membership in the Kuomintang, entered into cooperation with the CP which had been founded in 1921. In 1927 the Nationalists broke away from the Communists but retained the Leninist organisation of the party. The government, led by the Kuomintang, became wholly Western-oriented. A great part in this was played by Wang Ch'ung-hui, the internationally recognised legal

[18] Boorman and Howard, op. cit. (see p. 46, n. 15), under 'Wang Ch'ung-hui'; Escarra; pp. 109–12.
[19] Escarra, pp. 128–41; and Pan Wei-tung, *The Chinese Constitution: a Study of 40 Years of Constitution-making in China*, Washington DC, 1946, p. 48.

expert mentioned above. Next to him appeared a prodigious young legal genius, John Wu Ching-hsiung (Wu Jingxiong), who at the age of twenty-two was a student and friend of the eighty-year-old Justice Oliver Wendell Holmes in the United States, studied under the leading German legal authority Stammler in Berlin, and wrote an essay on international law in French in Paris. His writings won the highest praise from, among others, Justice Roscoe Pound, a great Americal legal authority.

Wu Ching-hsiung returned to China, not yet aged thirty, and became principal of the International Law School in Shanghai. In January 1933 the Nanking government decided to draw up a new constitution. A committee was established, but it was John Wu who single-handedly wrote the draft – and wrote it within a few weeks. It was published for dicussion and then passed with some modifications by the highest governing body of the Nationalist Party. On May 5, it was published as the final draft of the Constitution.[20]

There was no time to call a Constituent Assembly, because the Japanese forces were menacing North Chinese territories. In July 1937 the Japanese made an open attack on China. In November 1937 the Nationalist government moved from Nanking to Chungking. Not till November 1946, a year after the end of the war with Japan, was the National Assembly officially convened to vote on the Constitution. The Communists were invited but refused to attend. In March 1948 the first session of the National Assembly elected Chiang Kai-shek President. Wang Ch'ung-hui became head of the Judicial Yüan.[21] By then, however, China was already deep in civil war. In January 1949 the Communist troops entered Peking; in April they took the national capital, Nanking.

In the years immediately following the establishment of the Nanking government in 1928, the best lawyers were summoned to formulate not only the Constitution but laws for all branches of legal life where law applied. This was a continuation of the

[20] John C. H. Wu, *Beyond East and West*, London, 1952, and Ref. 14 above under 'Wu Ching-hsiung'.
[21] *China Handbook*, New York, 1950.

effort begun in the last years of the Ch'ing Dynasty and carried on through the turbulence of division in China. When the central government was established in Nanking in 1928, a Criminal Code was published at once, to be revised in 1935 after wide consultation. In 1929 a Civil Code appeared, followed by a number of legislative acts covering various aspects of the nation's life. This vast legislative effort laid the foundations of a modern China. It was clear that in this immense nation, with its age-old and close-knit traditions, the new laws could not be implemented overnight. The first paragraph of the civil law wisely stated that customary law is also a source of law as long as it is not at variance with public order.[22]

The nine years of international peace and growing internal pacification between the summer of 1928 and the outbreak of the Japanese war in the summer of 1937, were – in the judgment not only of foreign observers but also of average Chinese – the best period that China experienced in the twentieth century. During these years, the Supreme Court worked with great competence and its decisions were published as a guide for judges. Then came war – first the war with the Japanese invaders, then civil war – and the normal life of the country was suspended.

The legislation of the Nationalist government between 1928 and 1937 had been directed by highly skilled legal experts and was a remarkable endeavour to modernise the country. New ideas spread ever wider. But during the following years of international war and internal social and political disintegration, implementation of the laws became impossible, and the legislation of the late 1920s and early 1930s remained academic exercises scarcely affecting the majority of the population outside the modern cities. Traditional orderly legal life continued, however, in the hundreds of thousands of villages. Many of them, indeed, were exposed to the calamities of war and to harassment by local bandit groups. Yet, despite such interruptions, village life continued on its normal course. The explanation for this is to be found in the customary law, in age-old convictions of what is right and what is wrong, and in the traditional authority of the village heads.

[22] Escarra, p. 179.

The Confucianist consensus that had created an orderly social life was not broken. Family customs remained intact. Village teachers taught the children the traditional Confucianist morality of respect for authority and love of study, and they themselves wrote poems in ancient or modern styles. The illiterate population maintained their ancient tradition of civilised living, and were nurtured on stories of ancient heroes and ancient villains. In poorer villages only a few families would have any tools. These might disappear in the morning, a neighbour having borrowed them, but they would be returned faithfully in the evening.

In the war zones, atrocities by combatants were commonplace, and during the Japanese war railway lines were mined and trains derailed; but the stealing of railway, cable or telephone equipment or of any tools of public utility was unheard of, and the postal service, an ancient Chinese institution, remained intact, often having to pass through the front lines of battle. Customary law, of which the first paragraph of the 1929 Civil Law spoke, remained a vital part of the nation's life. Murder, rape and robbery were always exceptional aberrations in Chinese society.

This internal moral cohesion was broken up by the Communist regime.

3

THE MAO ERA: LAWLESSNESS

MAO AND LAW

Before 1949 two attempts had been made to introduce some sort of legality in Communist-dominated areas. In 1931 the Central Committee of the Communist Party (hereafter CP/CC) moved from Shanghai to Mao's camp in Juichin (Ruijin) in Kiangsi province. In that obscure corner of China some legal acts were published, under the direction of Moscow: Outline of the Constitution of the Chinese Soviet Republic, Land Law of the Chinese Soviet Republic, Labour Law of the Chinese Soviet Republic, Provisional Election Law of the Chinese Soviet Republic, Regulation on Punishment of Counter-revolutionaries in the Chinese Soviet Republic, Organisation Law of the Central Soviet of the Chinese Soviet Republic. That was the time before the great flight to the west, usually known as the Long March, when the Communists still expected a quick victory and the complete conquest of the country.

The second period of legislation was in the Yenan period. In 1935 the Communist troops arrived at Yenan in the north of Shensi province. When, two years later, the Japanese war erupted, the Communists joined the Nationalists in common resistance to the Japanese, but they were not ready to give up their independence.

Their small enclave round Yenan, the Shensi-Kansu-Ninghsia Revolutionary Base (Shanxi-Gansu-Ningxia), changed its name from Revolutionary Base to Border Area. In search of a reputation for respectability and civilised behaviour, an Assembly was elected in autumn 1937, immediately after the outbreak of the Japanese war. Early the following year, a Border Area government was set up and legislative acts were promulgated, among them a Marriage Law foreshadowing that of 1950. The head of the Area government was Lin Po-ch'ü (Lin Boqu), an old friend of Mao's since his young days. The Vice-Chairman was Kao Kang (Gao Gang), a local Communist leader whom Mao was to drive to commit suicide in 1954. The list of honorary Chairmen of the Assembly contained the names of Chiang Kai-shek, of some Nationalist generals and of Mao Tse-tung himself. The common front camouflage was perfect.[1] All power, however, remained in the hands of the Party leaders in Yenan. In the Communist history of those years, these democratic trappings are barely mentioned.

From 1942 to 1944, Mao's great thrust for power culminated in the violent inner-Party purge known as the Party Rectification. This led to the 7th Party Congress in 1945, and victory for Mao. Legal niceties became utterly unimportant.

In March 1927, when still a young man, Mao wrote of the peasant movement in his province, Hunan: 'A revolution is not a dinner party, or writing an essay, or painting a picture, or doing embroidery; it cannot be so refined, so leisurely and gentle . . . A revolution is . . . an act of violence by which one class overthrows the other.'[2]

At that time Mao knew little about Marxist theory, but what he said happened to be very Marxist indeed.

In June 1949 – he was then already in Peking – in his 'On the People's Democratic Dictatorship' Mao said: 'The State apparatus, including the army, the police and the courts, is the instrument by which one class oppresses another . . . It is violence and not benevolence.'[3]

On January 27, 1957, Mao addressing a conference of provincial Party committees said: 'The law must be observed and the revolutionary legal system must not be undermined. Laws form part of the superstructure. Our laws are made by the working people themselves . . . Counter-revolutionaries must be eliminated.

[1] Tsu Hai, *Li-shih fen-ts'e* 辭海（歷史分冊）(Fascicule on History) 1984; Wang Chiamin, *Chung-kuo kung-ch'an-tang shih kao* 王健民著：中國共產黨史稿 (Outline of the History of the Chinese Communist Party), T'aipei, 1965, vol. III, pp. 224 sq.; *Shen-Kan-Ning pien-ch'ü ta-shih-chi* 陝甘寧邊區大事記 (Chronology of Shen-Kan-Ning Border Area), Shensi, 1986.

[2] Report on an Investigation of the Peasant Movement in Hunan, in *Selected Works of Mao Tse-tung*, 5 vols, English edn, Peking, 1961–76, vol. 1 (pp. 23–62), p. 28.

[3] ibid., vol. IV (pp. 411–24), p. 418.

Where this task has not yet been completed according to plan, it must be completed this year.'[4] He then went on to expatiate on the need for getting rid of counter-revolutionaries.

For Mao law meant exterminating the counter-revolutionaries. A year earlier, in April 1956, in a speech to the Politburo, he had spoken openly about who should be killed. He had no legal scruples. 'In the early fifties, we executed a number of people . . . they were counter-revolutionaries.' Now, in 1957, fewer people were to be executed. Executions should continue, but 'those who are physically fit for manual labour should be reformed through labour . . . Counter-revolutionaries are trash, they are vermin, but once in your hands, you can make them perform some kind of service for the people.'[5] As in Russia, all major tasks were carried out by forced labour.

Under Mao, and after him, law was called 'the weapon of dictatorship'. The word Law stood for a threat. To be arrested meant that you positively were a criminal, because 'the People's Government cannot be wrong'. Felix Greene, an English admirer of Mao's regime, wrote that the Communist doctrine does not accept the independence of judges from the government. 'They claim that the government is the people, and that the people does not need to be protected from itself.'[6]

Mao Tse-tung died on September 9, 1976. Four years later, in 1980, there appeared a 188-page book summing up thirty years of legal history in Communist China. The book divided the thirty years from 1949 to 1979 into five periods:

1. *1949–1953.* In February 1949 – eight months before the establishment of the government of the People's Republic – all laws prevailing under the Nationalist government were annulled and the old judiciary system was abolished by a decision of the Party. In September a provisional Constitution known as the Common Programme was promulgated and courts were set up. In 1950 a marriage law, a trade union law and a land reform law were promulgated. In 1951 a regulation on suppression of

---

[4] ibid., vol. V (Chinese edn, Peking 1977, pp. 339–62), p. 359 f.
[5] ibid., vol. V., pp. 298–300.
[6] Felix Greene, *Awakened China: The country Americans don't know*, Doubleday, Garden City, NY, 1961, p. 193.

counter-revolutionaries and in 1952 a regulation on corruption were issued.

2. *1954–1957.* In September 1954 the first State Constitution of the PRC was enacted, accompanied by organic laws regulating state organs and the judiciary. Also a regulation on arrest and detention was published. In 1955 came a law on military service, and in 1957 a Decision on Labour Education – a new kind of forced labour.

3. *1958–1966.* Between 1959 and 1963, 420 decrees were published, among them a regulation on the protection of forests. The People's Congress published an Outline for Twelve Years' Development of Agriculture. But in all those nine years, 1958–66, not a single law was passed. Even some basic principles of the 1954 Constitution were exposed to official criticism. A number of comrades who defended legality were condemned as 'rightists'. 'Laws are odious; they tie the hands of the leaders.'

4. *1966–1976.* This was the time of the Cultural Revolution and the reign of the 'Gang of Four', a time of anarchy. There was no law and no legality.

5. The fifth period began after Mao died in 1976. As our book was published in 1980, it indicated only that a serious endeavour was being made to restore a sense of legality in life.[7]

This periodisation of the first thirty years of the Communist regime is correct. It shows that throughout that time there was only one short period of three years when an endeavour was made to introduce legality, even if this was Soviet legality. This came to an end in August 1957, with the introduction of a second type of forced labour, 'labour education' – the first type, 'corrective labour', had been introduced in the early 1950s. The vast land of China lived for thirty years in a legal vacuum.

THE START

The February 1949 Decision of the Communist Party – not of the government, which had not yet been set up – created the legal

---

[7] Lan Ch'üan-pu (ed.), *San-shih nien lai wo kuo fa-kuei yen-ke kai-k'uang* 藍全普編：三十年來我國法規沿革概況 (Survey of 30 Years' Development of Laws and Regulations in our Country), Peking, 1980.

vacuum by rejecting all previous legislation. In the Soviet Union too, immediately after the Revolution, pre-existing laws had been abolished and revolutionary tribunals had been set up to deal with counter-revolutionary cases. The difference was that in the Soviet Union a new criminal law was published in 1922, five years after the Revolution, and a civil code in 1923 whereas in China no criminal code was published until thirty years after the establishment of the People's Republic and no complete civil code has yet appeared at the time of writing, 1990.

At the end of 1986 a Shanghai monthly publication on law, *Fa-hsüeh* (Fa Xue, Jurisprudence), looking back at what happened in 1949, stated: 'Abrogating all previous laws meant that social life had no laws to rely on; this did not help the consolidation of proletarian dictatorship.'[8]

The Communist troops entered Peking at the end of January 1949. In February the courts and the prosecution offices of the Nationalist government were taken over. On March 18, courts-martial, called 'People's Courts', were set up in Peking. They came, so contemporary documents stated, under the military administration of the city and were to be instruments of 'people's democratic dictatorship'. Their purpose was the 'suppression of reactionaries and the restoration of the city's economic activities'.

In September 1949 the Common Programme, a provisional Constitution, was promulgated. Article 17 repeated what six months earlier had been decreed by the Communist Party, namely that all the laws and decrees and the judicial system of the Kuomintang 'reactionary government' were abolished and that new laws and decrees and a people's judiciary system were to be promulgated. Article 7 said that counter-revolutionary elements were to be suppressed and reactionary elements compelled to reform themselves through labour. This was the prelude to widespread killing of the 'class enemy' and to the institution of forced labour on a large scale.

A booklet written in November 1949 and published in March 1950 explained the situation. The judges were to study Mao's 'On

[8] *Fa-hsüeh* 法學, Shanghai, no. 6, 1986, pp. 18–19.

People's Democratic Dictatorship' with care. Dictatorship was to
be exercised and the enemies were not to be allowed to speak freely
or act freely. Now, it stated, there are no written laws or legal
codes. 'We do not rely on dead letters but on concrete policy; all
must act according to the stated policies.'

Then followed an instruction that court documents and verdicts
should not be written in the traditional legal style, but in colloquial simple language.

Newly-appointed judges, without legal training, could not
have written otherwise. Judges retained from former times – not
all could be dismissed at once – must have seen all too clearly that
times were changing.

There were too many cases and too few judges. In civilian cases
the courts acted as circuit courts and solved many disputes through
conciliation. In criminal cases the targets were evil landlords,
traitors (Kuomintang members) and heads of groups of households organised for self-defence by the previous government. 'The
masses are mobilised for accusation meetings; the courts accept the
accusations and pronounce sentence in front of the masses, and
the sentences are carried out on the spot' – this meant immediate
execution.

In a number of cases the accused refused to confess. They were
put 'under collective labour and ideological education' – collective
and individual discussions in which the government policy was
explained to them. Labour was not punishment but education;
labour combined with ideological education was meant to raise
their 'political consciousness'. If they behaved well, those who
had been sentenced to less than two years were allowed to return
home to sleep. Political education lasted three hours a day. The
detainees had to write down their reflections. In one such camp
in the summer of 1949 there were 729 inmates. In the morning
they got up at 6 a.m., had two hours' rest at noon, listened to
broadcasts (political themes) in the evening, and went to bed at
9 p.m. They got a daily ration of 22 ounces of *wu-wu-t'ou* (*wu-wo-
tou*, the roughest Chinese bread) and some vegetables. The problem was, as the booklet explained, that there was not enough
room for them. Twenty persons might be crammed into a small

space; the instructors themselves were ignorant men and women of little education.

The 1949 booklet quoted above contained several tables of statistics, showing how many cases were dealt with in various parts of the city. It described the situation in Peking before the formal establishment of the People's Republic, which took place on October 1.[9] The counter-revolutionaries were treated without mercy, but the old judges continued to behave in the way they had learned under the Nationalist government. This was a curious encounter of an old civilised judiciary with violent guerrilla methods brought to the city by uneducated Party cadres. The uneducated Party cadres won, and the following years witnessed an expansion of their methods – execution, forced labour and ideological indoctrination.

In the year after the establishment of Communist Party rule, three laws, mentioned above, were promulgated: the Land Reform Law,[10] the Marriage Law and the Trade Union Law.

The *Land Reform Law* was promulgated on June 30, 1950. On June 14, Liu Shao-ch'i (Liu Shaoqi), the second man in the Party hierarchy, had said: 'Land reform is an organised violent struggle. We rely on peasants and hired agrarian workers to destroy the feudal exploiting system.' Representatives are chosen, he said, from among the peasants, but the movement should be led by the Party cadres. Each county organises people's courts which circulate in the villages and lead the land reform. Liu recalled that the land reform carried out in the Communist-occupied areas in 1946–7 had led to incredible chaos. This was not to happen again. The masses were to be mobilised but were to be led by the Party men. The land of landlords and of all churches and temples was to be confiscated.

The Law said what Liu Shao-ch'i had said, adding that Buddhist monks and nuns, Taoists, Muslim leaders and Christian pastors were to be forced to labour. The Party men themselves led the

---

[9] *Jen-min ssu-fa kung-tso chü-yü* 人民司法工作舉隅 (A Glimpse of the Work of the People's Judiciary), Peking, 1950, 84 pp., with four tables.

[10] The Communist Party had twenty years' experience of land reform, suspended only in the time of cooperation with the Nationalist government during the Japanese war.

executions.[11] No official figures were ever given, but a pamphlet circulated internally thirty years later, in 1980, stated that the number of landlords and kulaks had fallen by 10.5 million.[12]

This may or may not indicate the number of those killed during the land reform. In the early 1950s there were still some foreign missionaries in the villages, and they reported daily executions. The peasants were gathered, landlords or enemies of the Communists were tied up and accused in violent scenes, and finally a soldier would shoot the condemned men in the back of the neck.

What did Mao Tse-tung think of the way the land reform was carried out? Thirty-eight years later, in 1987, a Peking magazine *Jen-wu* (Renwu; Personalities) published a long interview with the Professor Liang Shu-ming, by then ninety-four years old. He, together with many other intellectuals, had been sent to witness the land reform and thereby learn that class struggle was not a cocktail party. In 1951, Mao asked the professor what he thought of what he had seen. Prof. Liang replied that he had been shocked by the brutality he had seen – the landowners being cruelly beaten and some of them committing suicide. 'Chairman Mao smiled and said that such things had happened, but that not many landlords had committed suicide. The peasants' anger must be understood.'[13] Mao talked with Professor Liang several times. The two were born in the same year, 1893. In 1951 Mao reminded Liang that when he, Mao, was a minor clerk in the library of the Peking University, he used to open the door for Liang who at the age of twenty-four was already a lecturer at the University. Their fortunes had been reversed. Mao received him in audience several times. In 1955, however, Mao turned against him and the Chinese press published a spate of articles condemning the Professor.[14]

The *Marriage Law*, promulgated in May 1950, differed little from the Family Law of the Nationalist Government, promul-

[11] *The Agrarian Reform Law of the People's Republic of China*, Foreign Languages Press, Peking, 1950.

[12] *Kan-pu hsüeh-hsi ts'an-k'ao* 幹部學習參考資料 (Cadres Study Material), People's Broadcasting House, no. 1, 1980, 61 pp., p. 57 (for internal circulation only).

[13] *Jen-wu* 人物 , Peking, no. 2, 1987, p. 178.

[14] *China News Analysis* (hereafter CNA), Hong Kong, no. 111, Dec. 2, 1955, and no. 1981, June 3, 1977.

gated in 1930 in Section 3 of the Civil Code. In both, concubinage was treated as bigamy and marriage and the family were regulated on Western lines. The main novelty was that the 1950 Law prescribed registration as an essential constituent of marriage.

In reality, the 1950 Marriage Law turned out to be the basis of a political campaign, and an order was given that marriage reform should go hand in hand with the violent land reform. The old family system was to be broken down. Couples married in the old ways, under the guidance of their parents, should seek divorce. In popular language the Marriage Law was called the Divorce Law. Those who refused were treated as counter-revolutionaries and many women were handed over to the village militia, which soon became notorious for its licentious behaviour. Things went so far that two Cabinet Instructions, one in November 1952 and the other in February 1953, ordered a halt to the violence. In March 1953 an instruction from the Central Committee of the Communist Party said: 'Troubles of the past few years have been so serious and the reaction of people so unfavourable, that any further reforms would only aggravate the situation', and it ordered that the text of the Marriage Law should be communicated only to the regional and county leaders, and not to the uneducated lower ranks of the Party.[15]

In November 1953 it was stated officially that about 15 per cent of the population had accepted the family and marriage reform, 60 per cent were reluctant and 25 per cent had not yet been touched by the propaganda. A vice-chairman of the Committee for the Regulation of the Marriage Law Movement wrote: 'We erred gravely in not realising that . . . a feudalistic outlook on social customs still prevails among the masses.' The basis of the family reform was – as Lenin had said – that sex and the home are socialist concerns, not private ones. It had been expected that women released from family bondage would join the work-force; but the method used 'led to panic and serious social disturbances. Therefore the new tactics should be a long and patient education of the people'.[16]

[15] CNA, no. 5, Sept. 15, 1953.
[16] CNA, no. 15, Dec. 8, 1953.

The family reform, however, had one concrete result. The Communist cadres who went to the cities in 1949 left their village wives behind and married city girls – this became a popular joke in the Chinese cities.

The third Law of 1950 was the *Trade Union Law*. In the early 1920s the Communists dreamed of revolution in the cities and, in conjunction with the radical branch of the Kuomintang, organised violent industrial strikes there. After the break with the Kuomintang in 1927, they still hoped that, starting from their agrarian bases, they would be able to conquer the cities. In 1929 a secret trade union congress was held in Shanghai, and after that the Communists, squeezed out of the cities for twenty years, lost touch with the industrial workers. The next trade union congress was held in August 1948 in Harbin, Manchuria, which was already then under Communist rule. There it was decided that after the coming conquest of other parts of China had been accomplished, a national trade union should be set up.

On June 29, 1950, eight months after the establishment of the People's Republic, the Trade Union Law was promulgated. Its twenty-six articles showed Soviet influence. Encouraging competitive emulation between labour units for the fulfilment of production targets was prescribed, and the system of 'democratic centralism' was to be the rule. This meant centralised power with the democratic trappings of meetings and elections. The introduction of labour insurance was promised.

Four months later the Regulation on Labour Insurance was published. It offered advantages to employees of state-run enterprises, but beneficiaries had to go through political screening, carried out through 'struggle meetings', denunciations and other unpleasantness. The screening was carried out in parallel with the 'suppression of counter-revolutionaries' and was called 'democratic reform'.

COURTS AND JUDGES

In October 1950 the Cabinet issued an Instruction on legal work, signed by Chou En-lai (Zhou Enlai). It included an explicit statement of the Marxist principle 'Law is a tool for the oppression of one class by another'. It blamed government workers who were still using legal concepts that had been passed down from Nationalist times. 'We have not yet had time to pass new laws, but we have the Common Programme and the instructions of the government. The first task is the suppression of the counter-revolutionaries. We also have to deal with civil affairs, disputes among the people. People will have to be recruited from all fields and given rapid training in legal work.'

In January 1951 Lo Jui-ch'ing (Luo Ruiqing), Minister of Security, spoke of the task of the security organs: the suppression of counter-revolutionaries. He quoted a September 1950 Instruction of the Supreme Court – the new communist Supreme Court – and statements by Chou En-lai, urging severity and that there should be no gentle treatment of the enemy.

At the very beginning of the regime courts-martial were organised to deal quickly with the enemy. A regulation on these courts was published in July 1950, and an accompanying *People's Daily* editorial pointed out the distinction between People's Courts, called *Fa Yüan*, and these courts, called *Fa T'ing*. The *Fa T'ing* was an extraordinary court, a circuit court designed to arouse the masses – so that it might be apparent that it was not the government but the masses of the people who were condemning the class enemy. The *Fa T'ing* was a court-martial.[17]

P'eng Chen (Peng Zhen), the mayor of the city of Peking, said in February 1951: 'There are those who say that the people have already earned victory and that this should be a time for clemency and pardon.' To this the reply was 'no'; it had to be recognised that there were still many enemies about, and that they must be finished off.[18]

Two months later, on March 24 and 25, 1951, a mass accusation meeting was held in Peking. P'eng Chen, the mayor, stood before the emotionally worked-up audience and in a dramatic speech

[17] *Chien-chüeh chen-ya fan-ke-ming ho-tung* 堅決鎮壓反革命活動 (Resolutely Suppress Counter-revolutionary Activities), Peking, 1951.
[18] *Hsin-hua yüeh-pao* 新華月報 (hereafter *Hsin-hua Monthly*) no. 3, 1951, pp. 1000–1. In those days P'eng Chen was also deputy head of the Cabinet's Politico-Legal Committee.

asked them to pass sentence: 'Comrades, what should we do with all these criminals, bandits, secret agents, evil landlords, heads of reactionary Taoist sects?' The crowd unanimously roared: 'Shoot them'. The mayor continued: 'Should we be merciful to them?' 'No mercy', the crowd shouted back. The mayor commented: 'Truly, no mercy for them. If we pardoned them, that would be a sin on the part of the government.' The next question was: 'Is it cruelty to execute all these criminals?' The answer came back: 'It is not cruelty.' The mayor commented: 'Truly it is not cruelty. It is mercy. We are protecting the lives of the people whom they harm.' Then came the last question: 'Comrades, are they right or are we right?' And the last answer – 'We are right' – started off a wave of cheering for the mayor and Mao Tse-tung.

The mayor concluded: 'We are here representing the people. It is our duty to do the will of the people. We suppress the anti-revolutionaries. This act we perform according to the law. Those who have to be killed, we kill. In cases where we could kill or not, we do not kill. But when it has to be killing, we kill . . . Now you all want them to be suppressed. Tomorrow the Court will pronounce the judgment and they will be executed.'

The next day a big meeting was held outside the city walls and the executions took place and were broadcast over the radio.[19]

On February 21, 1951, when this bloody hunt for counter-revolutionaries and landlords – most of whom had only a few acres of land – had ended, the government Regulation on the Suppression of Counter-revolutionaries, signed by Mao Tse-tung, was published. It was a unique legal act, enumerating counter-revolutionary crimes to be punished by death or life sentences. Few legal documents in all history have succeeded in condensing into twenty-one articles so many offences punishable by death. Article 16, a gem of legal absurdity, said that the same sanctions should be imposed for crimes *not* enumerated.

P'eng Chen introduced a new legal concept, capital punishment with a two-year suspension of execution. The *People's Daily* explained that if the condemned showed signs of improvement

[19] *People's Daily* (*Jen-min jih-pao*, hereafter *PD*), Peking, April 3, 1951; *Hsin-hua Monthly*, April 1951, pp. 1238–40; *CNA*, no. 944, Dec. 23, 1973.

their sentence of capital punishment might be changed to a life sentence. 'This was not clemency,' P'eng said. 'The convicted left alive will not eat his food in vain; he will be forced to produce grain.'[20]

This institution was upheld throughout the years. When Chiang Ch'ing (Jiang Qing), Mao's widow, was condemned to death in 1981, the death penalty was imposed with a two-year suspension of execution. She was kept in prison und was not executed.

When the enemies, or potential enemies, had been exterminated – many more violent campaigns followed later – and the courts-martial had accomplished their work, the organisation of regular People's Courts began.

In September 1951 a Provisional Regulation decreed the establishment of People's Courts in three grades: in counties, in provinces and in Peking (the Supreme Court). These courts were to deal with criminal and civil cases, although there were no laws, except the Summary Provisional Constitution, the Common Programme of 1949, the Marriage Law, the Land Reform Law and the Trade Union Law. The country was still divided into six administrative areas ruled by military governments. A branch of the Supreme Court was to be set up in each area.[21]

The Minister of Justice, Shih Liang (Shi Liang), held a legal conference in August 1950 at which she revealed something that had not been mentioned openly elsewhere: participation by the Soviet Union. At the conference she said that there were two Russians who 'explained the Russian experience of legal work'.[22] In the early 1950s the Russians were everywhere.

In March 1951 the Minister of Justice said that some old judges were not severe enough; they did not understand that 'dealing with the enemies of the people is not clemency'.[23] Then, in 1952, the legal profession underwent a radical purge. On October 18, 1952, the *People's Daily*, quoting the Marxist axiom 'The law is

[20] *PD*, May 31, 1951; quoted in *CNA*, no. 56, Oct. 15, 1954.
[21] *Hsin-hua Monthly*, Sept. 1951, pp. 1010–12.
[22] *PD*, Nov. 5, 1950.
[23] *Hsin-hua Monthly*, March 1951, p. 1001.

the tool of the ruling class', said that formerly the Nationalists had been the ruling class; now the communists were. 'The two legal systems have nothing in common. The rotten capitalist legal theories must be eradicated.'

In practice this proved impossible. The Regulation on Punishment of Corruption used the old legal concepts of aggravating and extenuating circumstances, maximum-minimum penalties, cumulative crimes, and so on. The penalties themselves followed the old pattern: capital punishment, prison, a fine. But the old judges had gone.

In 1957 the same Minister of Justice, Shih Liang, said that in 1952 7 per cent, only 7 per cent, of the old lawyers had been punished; 70 per cent had been dismissed and had been given other jobs, though not in the legal field; and 20 per cent had been retained in legal work. To fill the vacant posts 'a great number of the revolutionary cadres have been entrusted with legal work. Thus the judiciary has become "pure". But now people say that the judges are legal ignoramuses.'

According to a *People's Daily* article published at the same time, '60–80 percent of the old lawyers were opposed to the Communist Party and many were actual enemies of the Party. The 1952 reform of the legal profession purged the old legal concepts.'[24] Twenty-six years after the publication of this article, in 1983, Ch'en P'ihsien (Chen Pixian), then head of the Politico-Legal Department of the CP/CC, wrote that before the Liberation, before the Communist take-over in 1949, there were 60,000 lawyers in China. Most of them were transferred to work outside the legal profession. Genuine legal experts were by then (in 1983) old, over eighty. In Shanghai, where Ch'en had once been first Party secretary, there were only 300 lawyers and these were very poorly paid, getting only 70 yüan a month.[25]

[24] *Kuang-Ming jih-pao* 光明日報 ('The Light Daily', hereafter *Kuang Ming Daily*), Peking, Oct. 6, 1957; *PD*, Oct. 14, 1957; CNA, no. 203, Nov. 1, 1957.
[25] *Min-chu yü fa-chih* 民主與法制 (Democracy and Legal System), Shanghai, no. 3, 1983.

EPHEMERAL LEGAL REFORMS

The year 1954 saw a great change in the legal life in China. The six regional Great Administrative Areas were abolished, and power was concentrated in Peking. A People's Congress, a sort of parliament, was convoked and approved a State Constitution. How all this came about, who were the initiators of this new move, is not clear even now. It may have been that Mao's companions thought it was time to settle down to normal administration of the country. More probably it was done at Soviet prompting – Soviet advisers were to be found everywhere in the central government. What is certain is that the Soviet system was taken as a model. The 1954 Chinese State Constitution, the first constitution of the People's Republic was modelled on the Soviet Union's 1936 Stalin Constitution. The preamble said that China was a republic and also a dictatorship, 'the People's Democratic Dictatorship'. The state had a chairman, who had no direct power. There was a single-chamber parliament, the People's Congress; its Standing Committee corresponded to the Presidium of the Soviet Union. There was a Cabinet, called a State Council, and there were people's courts and prosecutors' offices, which were declared 'independent'.

The courts were responsible to the corresponding governments on county and provincial level. The prosecutors' offices were to act on their own. However, all worked under the all-powerful Communist Party headed by Mao Tse-tung – who, up till 1959, also held the post of head of state.

There were some divergences from the Soviet Constitution. The Soviet Union was a federation of republics, whereas China is a 'unified, multi-national state'. In the Soviet Union the deputies of the parliament were elected by 'direct election' while China had indirect elections, the local people's congresses electing the county congresses, which elected the provincial congress, which in turn elected the members of the National Congress.

As in all Communist countries, the Constitution guaranteed a galaxy of freedoms, freedom of speech, of publication, of association, of demonstration, of change of domicile etc. As in the Soviet Constitution, one of the freedoms was religious freedom. Article

88 said: 'Citizens of the People's Republic of China enjoy freedom of religious belief.' The Soviet 'freedom of anti-religious propaganda' was omitted, the explanation being that 'the religious beliefs of the national minorities differ from those of the Han [Chinese] people.' Peking was concerned about adverse reaction among the Muslims and the Tibetans. The Soviet Constitution had freedom of 'religious cult'; in China 'religious ceremonies' was the term used: 'Religious ceremonies should not hinder production or hold up the execution of government orders.'[26]

In 1954 the government was organised, but there was as yet no sign of legislation on criminal or civil laws. There were instructions, Regulations and Ordinances – for instances the twenty-one-article Ordinance on Punishment of Counter-revolutionaries of February 21, 1951, mentioned above. Another ordinance was published when the violent campaign against corruption was approaching its end, the 18-article Punishment of Corruption promulgated on March 24, 1952. Both were published as the campaigns came to their ends. Both had retroactive force.[27]

In 1956 the first signs of criticism of the Soviet system appeared. Stalin had died in March 1953, but he was only exposed in 1956, at the 20th Soviet Party Congress, by Khrushchev. China adjusted to the changing atmosphere in the Soviet Union. The Communists in China had been nurtured for years on the 'Short Course of the History of the Communist Party in the Soviet Union (Bolshevik)', the bible of the Stalinist regime. Now this was exposed to criticism in the Soviet Union, and economists in China expressed regret that for years their books on the economy had been mere translations from Russian.[28]

In 1957 was the notorious 'free speech', when Mao called upon the intellectuals to express criticism of the Communist Party. When they obeyed, he sent them to a new type of labour camp, the Labour Education Camps. Much of what distinguished jurists

[26] PD, June 15, 1953, quoted in CNA, no. 1, June 25, 1954; Ta kung pao 大公報, T'ienchin, June 23, 1954, qoted in CNA, no. 45, July 23, 1954.
[27] Chung-hua jen-min kung-he-kuo fa-kuei mu-lu 中華人民共和國法規目錄 (List of Laws and Regulations of the People's Republic of China), Peking, 1984, 314 pp.
[28] PD, Aug. 5, 1956; Kuang Ming Daily, Sept. 7, 1956, quoted in CNA, no. 156, Nov. 9, 1956.

and others had said in the 'free speech' period, or were alleged to have said, was published in the second half of 1957, when the incautious speakers were condemned as 'rightists' and punished. An adviser of the Supreme Court had been bold enough to say that lawyers of the old regime were being sent to work as 'coolies in hospitals and crematoria' and that the newly-promoted 'judges' were unable to write their verdicts: when passing sentence they simply copied out the confessions of the defendants and added some such phrase as 'committed a great and evil crime'.

A court verdict, a copy of which was brought out of China, sentenced a Christian student to fifteen years. The verdict enumerated her crimes: 'She helped the church, and she even said that she was ready to carry the cross until she died.' She had been sentenced by one of these ignorant judges.

Legally-trained men, even inside the Communist Party, had observed this development with consternation. Some men in the Ministry of Justice were quoted as having said 'Today there is only policy; there is no law.' They received their answer: there were laws – laws on counter-revolutionaries and trade unions, a marriage law, a regulation on the people's police, and so on. During the eight years of the regime since 1949, 4,072 legislative acts had been passed. This answer did not point out that most of these were internal circulars, executive orders or instructions.

A well-known Shanghai lawyer, Ku Chih-chung (Gu Zhizhong) said that the Constitution existed merely in name – Article 85, for example, 'Citizens of the People's Republic of China are equal before the law' or Article 89, 'No citizen may be arrested except by the decision of the People's Courts or with a warrant of the People's Prosecution Yüan', or Article 87 which decreed 'freedom of speech, freedom of the press, of assembly, of association'. These things are on paper only, he said. 'Everybody, from the Committee Chairman Liu [Shao-ch'i] down to the ordinary citizen, considers the Constitution a useless piece of paper.' Even the president of the criminal division of the Supreme Court, Chia Ch'ien (Jia Qian), had become a 'rightist'.

The reversal of the free speech policy was total. In the summer of 1957 at the annual meeting of the People's Congress, Chou

En-lai rejected the liberal views produced during the free speech period. To the complaint that there were no laws he replied – revealing this for the first time – that the draft of a criminal code was ready and that work was under way on drafts of a civil code and of a code of public security. At the 1959 session of the People's Congress the Supreme Court report said that consultations had been carried out in 1955–6 on the writing of a criminal and a civil code. In 1958, however, the Great Leap Forward came, and there was no longer any need for these drafts.[29]

The whole legal profession was purged once again. A monthly paper, *Research in Politics and Law*, said in its April 1959 issue that there were lawyers who were pleading for stability and precise legislation. This, they were told, was an illusion: 'Law cannot be defined precisely, for objective reality is too complicated, it develops and changes indefinitely. Laws would tie the hands and feet of the Party workers and of the masses, and would handicap both the fight against the enemy and the development of production . . . The law of our country is a changing law adapted to the perpetual revolution . . . Since the policy of the Party is the soul of the legal system, legal work is merely the implementation and execution of the Party's policy . . . It would be a great mistake to have fixed parliaments and unchanging rules which would hinder the revolutionary struggle.'

This review itself changed hands. Having been founded in 1953 by the Chinese Political and Legal Association, it was taken over in 1959 by the Law Research Institute of the Academy of Sciences, set up in October 1958. Six well-known lawyers were expelled from the Legal Association, among them its President Ch'ien Tuan-sheng (Qian Duansheng).[30] The programme of the reorganised review was 'to propagate the doctrines of Marxism-Leninism, the Thoughts of Mao Tse-tung, and Party policy documents concerning state and law'.[31]

The events of 1954–6, the time when some legality was introduced, even if it was only Soviet legality, looked now like distant

[29] *CNA*, nos 187, July 5, 1957, and 284, July 10, 1959.
[30] Born 1900, a LL.D of Harvard University.
[31] *CNA*, no. 284, July 10, 1959.

dreams. In the spring of 1959 the Vice-President of the Republic Tung Pi-wu (Dong Biwu), the Foreign Minister Ch'en Yi (Chen Yi) and other distinguished persons led a meeting of Advanced Legal Workers. The legal workers promised to 'obey the Party committees, rely on the popular masses and take part in productive labour'. To labour they went! In some provinces all legal workers in the courts were sent to the villages to till the land, administering justice only in their free time under the supervision of the local Party committees. In some places the public were told how much dung the judges had collected in how many working days, and how many legal cases they had adjudicated. They were 'eating, living and working together with the peasants'. 'Eating together, becoming one with the masses, is the necessary prerequisite for the guidance of the masses by the Party.'[32]

THE 'SIXTIES AND 'SEVENTIES

Legal work was at a standstill. The disruption of the economy through the introduction of the People's Communes and the craze of the 'Great Leap Forward' caused nation-wide famine – a fact not admitted in Peking until twenty years later. The country was on its knees and the Party, paralysed, did not dare to act, and instead withdrew into its shell.

Party control having weakened, the intellectuals were able to speak more freely. It was in those days that the universities began to praise Confucius and the Confucian humanistic ethics. In Peking the review *Research in Politics and Law* plucked up courage and joined with the law departments of the major universities to hold theoretical discussion meetings. The debates were led by Chang Yu-yü (Zhang Youyu), head of the Legal Research Institute and Vice-President of the Chinese Association for Politics and Law.[33] Even now they did not dare to speak freely. All said that Party policy was more important than law. 'The policy of the

---

[32] *PD*, May 23, and July 21, 1959; *CNA*, No. 397, Nov. 17, 1961; *PD*, Sept. 17 and 18, 1960; *CNA*, No. 344, Oct. 14, 1960.

[33] Born 1899 and entered the Party in 1927. In the 1980s he was still playing a leading role.

Party is the soul of law, and law is the tool for implementing the policy.' All exalted the Party will. Yet these lawyers still used legal language, speaking of Law, Decree, Decision and Order and discussing which organ had the power to create laws or decrees, and so forth.

They discussed the well-known Maoist division of Chinese society into those 'within the People' and those 'without' – the outcasts. Some said that those 'within the People' observe the law spontaneously, and that the others need coercion. This strangely resembled the ancient Chinese legal system, which distinguished between the upper and lower classes.

The lawyers in Shanghai had another approach. They did not discuss law as it was, or was not, in those days, but worked instead on re-editing ancient dynastic histories, with emphasis on the legal codes of the T'ang Dynasty. T'ang law, it was explained, had clear statements on crimes and sanctions; the accused were given chances to defend themselves, and if the judges themselves did not observe the law, they were punished by flogging.

All this was written about ancient Chinese law, but the point was obvious: in China at the present time there were no longer any legal codes, any laws according to which the judges could act, or any restraint on illegal acts.

The newspapers even published essays on Western classics on legal theory. Several articles appeared on Montesquieu and the separation of legislature, administration and judiciary. They said, of course, that Montesquieu was wrong: in Marxist society there is division of work but no division of power. They quoted Mao: 'The law is the expression of the will of the ruling class.' Yet at least the readers learnt something about Montesquieu and about separation of power, of which nothing had been said before.

In 1961 the Commercial Press published a translation of Hegel's *Philosophy of Law*. A reviewer in the *People's Daily* condemned Hegel; but at least Hegel had been published in Chinese. An essay appeared about the French law professor Léon Duguit who criticised Marxism and condemned class struggle. Duguit, of course, was wrong; but the reader learnt something.

Even the Pure Law Doctrine (*Reine Rechtslehre*) of the Viennese

Hans Kelsen was discussed. An essay in the *People's Daily* said that Kelsen, a positivist, separates law from morals and law from justice, condemning the Communist theory of law and saying that there is a contradiction between the Marxist theory of the state and the Marxist theory of law. The *People's Daily* naturally did not like this and said that Kelsen had made a poisonous attack on Marxism and 'rechanted the old songs of bourgeois scholars'. Kelsen holds that all positive law is built upon a fundamental hypothesis, the power of the state; thus he 'defends, by such abstract logic, the interests of the reactionary monopolists'. He says – under the influence of American law, for in his later years he taught in the United States – that even the courts can create law. This means that there is not even a consistent bourgeois law and that the working class cannot defend itself by relying on written law. Kelsen proposes a world government and denies the sovereignty of individual states. The answer to this is, 'All know that the sovereignty of the state is one of the fundamental principles of modern international law' – a strange answer from a Marxist, who was supposed to believe in international solidarity.

On the surface, all these essays defended Marxism. But there had been an airing of Western legal theories that had never been presented to Chinese readers since 1949 – and were not to be heard of again in the following seventeen years.[34]

In September 1962 the wind changed and Mao Tse-tung succeeded in reimposing his will at the Central Committee meeting. The years of the Cultural Revolution were approaching. Mao was in a radical mood. The cultural world was purged, and a large-scale purge began in the villages. Chiang Ch'ing, Mao's wife, radicalised the theatre. The United Front Department of the Party, which controlled the national minorities, was found to be too moderate and was disbanded. Lin Piao was transforming his military forces into a political fighting power. The Cultural Revolution began in the summer of 1966, when millions of Red Guards, swearing fidelity to Mao and Lin Piao, launched into their orgy of vandalism. They spent August/September 1966

[34] For detailed references see *CNA*, no. 467, May 10, 1963.

plundering the homes of middle-class families, burning books, breaking *objects d'art* and destroying Christian churches and Buddhist temples. This was lawlessness organised from above. Not all houses, but only those designated from above were plundered, and the stolen property was handed over at collection centres. Some twenty years later much of this loot was returned to the original owners or their descendants, or nominal compensation was paid for things lost.

In that summer of 1966, people dubbed 'bourgeois' were beaten up, tortured and paraded in the streets. On the approach of the Red Guards many educated people such as professors and writers, who had served the government for years, committed suicide. Their reputations were rehabilitated between fifteen and twenty years later. At the end of 1966 the hordes of the Red Guards, still directed by Lin Piao's soldiers, turned against Party leaders. These tough old guerilla fighters, unlike the professors and writers, did not commit suicide, but many of them, including Liu Shao-ch'i, the Number Two man in the Party, died in prison.

By 1967 the Red Guards, organised throughout the country in violent fighting groups, had got out of control. The army was sent to restore order – and failed to do so. Various army units supported one or another Red Guard group in province-wide fighting. Chaos was total. The provincial Party organisations were smashed and youngsters wearing 'Red Guards' armbands and with revolvers at their belts were taking over the running of cities. Young workers joined them. Chaos indeed!

Law, in any intelligible sense, was at an end. Rebel organisations took it into their own hands, arresting people and setting up their own courts. In 1968 mass trials were held with, in some places, 100,000 people present. In one case it was said that the executions had been approved by the Supreme Court in Peking.[35] In a small town in the north-west of China, a mass trial condemned a man 'with the permission of a higher legal organ'. 'The will of the revolutionary people was strengthened and proletarian dictatorship consolidated', the provincial radio announced.[36]

[35] Chekiang Radio, Sept. 11, 1968; *CNA*, no. 731, Nov. 1, 1968.
[36] Shensi Radio, Sept. 11, 1968; *CNA*, no. 793, March 6, 1970.

Before the Cultural Revolution, the rule had been that permission of the Supreme Court had to be obtained before a capital sentence could be carried out. But in those years the Supreme Court was rarely mentioned. The courts, like everything else, were ruled by the military.

Often justice was administered by mass organisations which were themselves engaged in fighting other mass organisations. Human life counted for nothing. In 1968 the public in Hong Kong were shocked when bodies, mutilated or with hands tied, were seen floating down the river from the neigbouring Kuangtung province.

Ever since the beginning of the Cultural Revolution the fiercest of the insurgents had been secondary school students, especially girls. A leaflet published by Peking schoolchildren said: 'We will fight anyone who is opposed to the proletarian line of our Party. He will die and we shall live. What the former generations have gained by sweat and blood we will continue to protect, maintaining the tradition for ever! We lift high the great banner of class-line! Thousands of martyrs sacrificed themselves before us for the good of the people. Let us raise high their banner and go forward along their path of blood!'[37]

Throughout the Cultural Revolution this Blood System, the theory that 'only social origin counts', incited fighting groups against one another. This was the battle-cry of the children of the privileged classes who had gathered into powerful organisations to fight the enemy. The enemies were the children of the 'bourgeois' and the downtrodden – the 'landlords, kulaks, counter-revolutionaries and bad elements' – outcasts from the early days of the People's Republic.

The villages also were in uproar. Young peasants rushed off to the cities to fight. They were not interested in the great political issues. As a statement quoted from the mountainous Kueichou province put it: 'There are thousands of mountains and rivers between us and Liu Shao-ch'i [who had been condemned]. We are illiterate. That is the business of those who know how to read and write.'

[37] CNA, no. 636, Nov. 11, 1966.

The outcast elements in the villages remembered well what land and which houses had belonged to their families before the land reform; and the state found it difficult to collect taxes in the villages. Some villages made money by bringing eggs, peanuts and other farm products to the cities and selling them at high prices. Old feuds between village clans broke out once more and the villagers claimed the graves of their ancestors.[38]

The chaos was total. Hordes of Red Guards were roving through the country fighting for power. The security organs, police and other bastions of public order collapsed. So did the courts and the procurators' offices. All were taken over by the military and combined under the name 'kung-chien-fa' (gongjianfa), which meant Security-Procuration-Courts.

Oddly enough, Hsieh Fu-chih (Xie Fuzhi), the Minister of Security, did not fall. He had taken over the post in 1959 from Lo Jui-ch'ing, leader of the terrible purges in the 1950s, who became chief-of-staff at the same time as Lin Piao became Minister of Defence. Lin Piao took over from P'eng Te-huai (Peng Dehuai) whom Mao had purged. During the Cultural Revolution Lo Jui-ch'ing was arrested by the Red Guards and declared a counter-revolutionary. To escape, he jumped out of a window and broke a leg. Red Guard tabloids had a picture of him with one leg in plaster. After the death of Lin Piao in September 1971, Lo returned to a high position. He died in 1978. He was obviously not a friend of Lin Piao.

By contrast his successor, Hsieh Fu-chih, who had taken over the security portfolio in 1959, was not touched by the Cultural Revolution. Indeed he became concurrently head of the Peking Revolutionary Committee and deputy head of the army's Cultural Revolution Team. During the Cultural Revolution he, the Minister of Security, destroyed the security along with the pro-curations and the courts. A Red Guard tabloid of those days quoted him as saying that Chairman Mao wanted to smash security, procuration and courts, for 90 per cent of the security bureau were supporting the old guard. Hsieh's own words were:

[38] *CNA*, nos 679, Sept. 29, 1967, and 729, Oct. 18, 1968.

'It may sound odd that I, Minister of Public Security, am speaking against the Public Security. However, this is a reminder that one must follow Chairman Mao and Vice-Chairman Lin and not the conservatives.'[39]

In March 1971, Lin Piao was still alive and Hsieh remained the Party boss of Peking. In the following year Hsieh died, and six years later, in 1978, as the rule of Teng Hsiao-p'ing (Deng Xiaoping) was beginning, he was condemned posthumously along with Lin Piao. In 1980, a Party decision invalidated even the speech delivered at Hsieh's funeral in 1972; it was not mentioned that the funeral speech had been delivered by Chou En-lai.

During the Cultural Revolution large 'rebel' groups set up their own forced labour camps, locking up members of opposing groups and condemning their enemies in summary judgment. Then the military took over security-procuration-courts. All this created chaos in the country and destroyed the very idea of organised justice. Mao had always despised orderly legal life.

However, in 1970 there were signs of a desire for a return to some species of legality. A Draft State Constitution was drawn up and was discussed throughout the country. News of this was brought out by visitors from China, and the text was published in Taiwan. The authenticity of the text was proved by the use that the Chinese mass media began to make of terms which had first appeared in the Draft. Then nothing happened. The Draft had been shelved.

The Draft Constitution exalted Lin Piao's role. Article 26 stated: 'The most fundamental rights and duties of citizens are to support Chairman Mao Tse-tung and his close comrade-in-arms Vice-Chairman Lin Piao.' The Draft Constitution was drawn up with military brevity. It consisted of thirty articles, whereas the 1954 Constitution had had 106. It made Mao the 'permanent head of state'. In a single article it dealt with courts, including the Supreme Court and the regional courts – all of which were to be responsible to the People's Congresses at the same level. There was

[39] *CNA*, nos 742, Jan. 31, 1969, and 762, June 27, 1969.

no mention of a Supreme People's Procuratorate.

At the time when the Draft Constitution was being discussed throughout the country, events took a dramatic turn. From August 23 to September 6, 1970, a Party CC Plenum was held at Lushan, a summer resort in Kiangsi province. This was the second Plenum since the 1969 Party Congress, which had made Lin Piao successor-designate to Mao. At the Lushan meeting Mao turned against Ch'en Po-ta (Chen Boda), who had been his intimate companion and his ghost-writer since the Yenan days and who, during the Cultural Revolution, had been made head of the Cultural Revolution Team. The Lushan meeting was held in secret, and the case of Ch'en Po-ta became clear only in the following year. That Mao at the same meeting had turned sharply against Lin Piao himself was not made public till months after Lin Piao's death in September 1971. The Draft Constitution exalting Lin Piao was buried.

The chaos did not abate with the end of the Cultural Revolution or with the never fully explained death of Lin Piao. The strife between Chou En-lai and his old guard, on the one side, and the radicals of Chiang Ch'ing, Mao's wife, on the other, still continued. In January 1975 a People's Congress was held, the first since January 1965. A new State Constitution was promulgated after presentation by the radical Chang Ch'un-ch'iao (Zhang Chunqiao); it was a revised version of the 1970 Draft. This 1975 text explained what had happened to the procuratorates. In the 1954 Constitution, arrest was supposed to be made by 'the decision of the people's court or with the sanction of the people's procuratorate'. The new Constitution said: 'No citizen may be arrested except by decision of the people's court or with the sanction of a public security organ.' The security sector took over the functions of the procuratorate. The Minister of Security was Hua Kuo-feng, who in April 1976, five months before the death of Mao, became Prime Minister and, after Mao's death, Chairman of the Communist Party.

The Constitution of 1975 was short-lived; a month after Mao's death Chiang Ch'ing and her radicals were arrested. In March 1978 a third State Constitution was enacted, to be followed in

1982, when Teng Hsiao-p'ing was already in the saddle, by a fourth.

The 1978 Constitution returned to the form of the 1954 one, which had been inspired by the Soviet model. The office of the procurator or public prosecutor, suppressed in 1975, was restored, but the statement in the 1954 Constitution that 'the people's courts are independent, subject only to the law' was omitted. This Constitution still spoke of landlords, kulaks, bad elements and counter-revolutionaries, and added two new 'elements': 'reactionary capitalists and new-born bourgeois elements who resist socialism and embezzle public goods'.

The 1978 Constitution did not bring peace and order. Many reports told of abuses – local Party leaders setting up their own private tribunals, the use of torture, forced confessions. Characteristically, the offenders were not punished by the courts but were given Party punishments which ranged from admonition to expulsion from the Party. It was made clear that no Party member might be summoned to court without first being expelled from the Party. A Party member enjoys the equivalent of what in Western countries is known as parliamentary immunity; this has always been the practice in the People's Republic and it remained so in the 1980s.[40]

---

[40] *CNA*, no. 1121, June 2, 1978.

4

AFTER MAO

FOR LEGALITY

At the 1978 People's Congress, held in February-March, Hua Kuo-feng, head of the Party and Premier, spoke of the need for what he called the Socialist Legal System. 'It is essential to strengthen the Socialist Legal System if we are to bring order into the country. We should draw upon our twenty-eight years of experience of the dictatorship of the proletariat, give a ready ear to opinions of the masses, and gradually enact our Socialist laws and then perfect them.'

Shortly after the People's Congress, articles in the *People's Daily* appeared, containing things that had not been seen or heard for more than twenty years. One of these articles was written by a seventy-year-old lawyer, Han Yü-t'ung (Han Yutong), a Party member and the wife of the similarly well-known lawyer, Chang Yuyü (Zhang Youyu), mentioned above. 'For many years', she wrote, 'legislation did not exist. Badly-needed laws were not drawn up, regulations in need of revision were not revised . . . There are people who worry and dare not mention the problem of making, implementing and observing laws . . . For the strengthening of the socialist legal system a start must be made with wide-ranging legislative work. Experiments in this field must be collected, and criminal and civil laws drawn up.'[1]

Hers was the first voice in Peking to declare that the People's Republic had lived in a legal vacuum, that legislation – even as it existed in other Communist countries – was non-existent. The country had been ruled by the arbitrary will of the masters and by inner departmental regulations and instructions which had not been made public.

Towards the end of 1978, the *People's Daily* said that for many years the error had been widespread that Party policy can take the

[1] *PD*, March 16, 1978.

place of law. The result was that neither criminal nor civil law
was taught in the law faculties of the universities, but only Party
policy – Policy of Criminal Cases and Policy of Civil Cases and the
like. No theory of law was taught, but only Party Guidance and
the Line of the Masses. 'Law students studied law for four years,
but learned nothing about law. [. . .] 'The sayings of Mao became
law, and the verdicts of the courts quoted not laws but the Sayings
of Chairman Mao. We have not even criminal laws or criminal
procedural laws. The courts have the Party Line, directives and
Party policy, no laws.'

'There are people who believe that laws are not necessary,
that it is enough if the leading comrades of the Party committees say a word. In fact, courts adjudicate cases and impose sanctions, guided merely by a word or an instruction from a leading
comrade. [. . .] Many of the regulations issued by various organisations say merely: "Those who contravene these regulations
will be punished according to the law" – but according to what
law?'

These were brave words. But what law meant was still not
clear. It was pointed out that for a Party leader to decide a legal
case as he wished was wrong. The remedy proposed was that
'important questions should be decided by a collective discussion
of a Party committee, not by one man alone', and it was still
solemnly stated that 'Party policy is the soul of law, and law is
the tool for the expression of Party policy'.

What law actually was fell into oblivion. 'As nobody has talked
about law for many years, the concept of law, even elementary
notions of law, are not present in people's minds. But there is no
precedent in the history of China or any country in the world for
a state existing without laws.'

While saying this, the *People's Daily*, though apparently defending the rule of law, declared that 'law is the tool of one class for
ruling over the other . . . Laws are the tools of dictatorship. If
there are no laws, as happened under Lin Piao and the Gang of
Four, people's houses can be destroyed – as was done by the Red
Guards – people can be arrested, imprisoned, beaten to death or

subjected to fascist torture. Good cadres and masses[2] suffered this way. Can we forget this?'[3]

Before the Cultural Revolution, the 'masses' had been condemned without any law, and the Party leaders had found this quite normal; in good Marxism one class suppresses the other class. But when the Party leaders themselves were exposed to the same treatment during the Cultural Revolution, they began to ponder the absurdity of the situation.

This awakening to the necessity of having some laws to live by appeared in the national press with greater emphasis at the end of 1978, when Teng Hsiao-p'ing was on the way up and his reform thoughts were spreading openly through the country.

In June 1978 Teng was already speaking with authority at the Army's Political Work Conference. He demanded punishment for those who had committed crimes during the Cultural Revolution. This was a difficult demand to put into practice. Some Party leaders were afraid that it might be interpreted as 'opposition to the great banner of Chairman Mao'. As the *People's Daily* said in July 1978: 'There are some Party committee leaders who wonder whether a new turn of events will not come and whether they will not be called "rightist" when that happens. Often the very men who condemned the comrades have now to rehabilitate them. Does this not mean the negation of oneself?'[4]

At the same time a process began for the rehabilitation of those who had suffered unjustly under the rule of the radicals. Some cases were easy to deal with. The court in Nanking city found people in labour camps who, having inadvertently destroyed a picture of Mao, had been condemned as counter-revolutionaries. A dock-worker had once said, when looking at a picture of Mao and Lin Piao, that the Chairman had a shiny face and that Lin Piao looked like a thin stick. He was declared a counter-revolutionary and jailed. A worker wrote a wallposter denouncing Liu Shao-ch'i. At the time the Cultural Revolution itself was busy

[2] 'Masses' are the non-Party-members.
[3] PD, Nov. 7, and 24, 1978.
[4] PD, July 9, 1978.

denouncing him, but the worker wrote a wrong character and got
seven years.

Many cases were not so simple. Chiang Hua (Jiang Hua), President of the Supreme Court, declared that the judges were afraid
to review unjust sentences. Hsü Chia-t'un (Xu Jiatun), then first
Party secretary of Kiangsu province, said that the judges were
afraid to act when, as sometimes happened, the original verdict
condemning a man had been given by the very man who now had
the duty of reviewing erroneous judgments. This, Hsü said, puts
a man in an awkward position.[5]

CRIMINAL CODE

In July 1979, at the yearly session of the People's Congress, P'eng
Chen, then head of the Legislative Commission of the People's
Congress, introduced a Criminal Code consisting of 192 Articles,
divided, according to the Western style, into a General Part and
a Special Part. For a Communist country, this was a reasonable
piece of legislation. P'eng Chen, who for forty-odd years had been
a leading personality in the Party and had led the execution of the
counter-revolutionaries in Peking in the early 1950s, became the
champion of legality. In so doing, he did not change much. When
introducing the new law at the People's Congress, he said: 'The
people's security organs, the people's procuratorate and the people's courts are the tools of the proletarian dictatorship for the
protection of the people and for dealing severe blows to the
enemies.'

Article 1 of the Criminal Code declared that the Law follows
Marxism-Leninism and Mao Tse-tung's Thought, the people's
democratic dictatorship and proletarian dictatorship – two names
for the same thing. Article 2 said that the task of the Criminal
Code is to struggle against counter-revolutionary criminal acts
and to protect proletarian dictatorship, the wealth of the 'whole
people' (i. e. state properties) and of the collectives, citizens' property and their personal, democratic and other rights. Article 80

[5] Kiangsu Radio, Oct. 4, 1978.

specified that in cases where the existing law was not appropriate to national minorities, the autonomous areas might propose special regulations to the People's Congress Standing Committee.

That Chinese invention, capital punishment with two years suspension – explained first by P'eng Chen in the early 1950s – was retained, and so was the ancient Chinese institution of self-denunciation, rewarded in the law by reduction or remission of sanctions. The Criminal Code is severe on popular religious practices, which are described as 'feudal superstition'. Article 147 says that infringement by state officials of freedom of religion is punishable by a maximum of two years in prison or detention, but this refers only to religious bodies organised under the tutelage of the government. 'Those who use or organise feudal superstition' – popular, unorganised, religious practices – may be punished by up to a minimum of five years in prison (Article 99).

The Criminal Code was generous in granting the number of offenses for which capital punishment could be imposed. Among these was causing serious damage to factories, stores, residential areas and so on, for murder and rape, for embezzlement of public property by state employees, and for a whole range of 'counter-revolutionary crimes', ranging from conspiring with a foreign power to mob irruption into prisons, damaging river banks, robbing public archives, stealing goods from industrial or mining enterprises, hijacking ships, airplanes or cars, and fabricating or stealing weapons or ammunition. The law approved (in Article 79) the use of analogy, which meant that an action not listed in the law might also be treated as criminal by analogy.

Lawyers in China knew that modern legal systems do not allow the use of analogy. One lawyer, T'ao Hsi-chin (Tao Xijin), in a talk explaining the Criminal Law, said that the law allowed the use of analogy because of the huge size of China and the diversity of conditions. He did, however, say that the use of analogy required a permit from the Supreme Court.[6] Whether this was his personal view or referred to an internal instruction is not clear.

Shortly after the publication of the Criminal Code, a pro-

---

[6] *Fa-hsüeh yen-chiu* 法學研究 (Studies in Law), no. 5, Peking, 1979, summarised also in *PD*, Jan. 15, 1980, p. 5.

Peking monthly in Hong Kong asked: 'Will these laws remain
on paper only?' Article 144 decrees that illegal imprisonment of
a person and illegal entry into people's houses could be punished
by maximum three years in prison or detention. Would this stop
the abuses?

The Criminal Code said nothing specific about forced labour
camps, only that prison sentences might last from six months to
fifteen years and be served either in prison or in a corrective labour
camp (Articles 40–41). Four months after the promulgation of
the Criminal Code, the People's Congress Standing Committee
declared that labour education camps, introduced in 1957, were
to continue.

The Criminal Code and the Criminal Procedural Law promulgated in July 1979 were supposed to come into force on January
1, 1980. In February, however, the People's Congress Standing
Committee delayed the implementation of the laws for the simple
reason that the courts, procuratorates and security organs had not
yet been re-established and there was a lack of personnel.

It was decreed that the old criminal procedural law was to be
observed. However, there had been no such law before. 'For a
long time', a *Kuang Ming Daily* article in Peking said in October
1979, 'those who had been working in the legal profession were
sent to work in the fields, and few who are now working in the
legal departments have had any legal training.' A vacuum lasting
between two and three decades cannot be filled in an instant.
There were no books on law in the bookshops and it was hard
to find even the texts of recent legislation. In 1957 there were
2,800 lawyers in China. Many of them had been condemned as
'rightists' in that year, and ten years later during the Cultural
Revolution many were branded as counter-revolutionaries and
sent to labour camps. Towards the end of the 1970s, the universities had begun to teach law, with a total enrolment of 2,000
students.[7]

Three months after the promulgation of the Criminal Code in
October 1979, a young man, Wei Ching-sheng (Wei Jingsheng),

[7] *Kuang Ming Daily*, Oct. 24, 1979.

appeared in a televised court hearing, accused of having sold military secrets about the war on the Vietnam border, slandered Mao Tse-tung's Thought in *The Search*, a magazine he had founded himself, and called proletarian dictatorship 'feudal absolutism under the cloak of socialism'. He was given a fifteen-year prison sentence. The Criminal Code, in spite of having been promulgated, had not yet come into its full vigour. He was judged and sentenced under the odious 1951 Regulation on Suppression of Counter-Revolutionaries, which meted out forced labour and death to millions.[8]

He was not the first to be arrested, but his became the *cause célèbre*. He was the victim of the short-lived enthusiasm of the young for the new Teng era early in 1979. The new freedom was tolerated, even encouraged. On January 11, 1979 in the *People's Daily* a specially – invited Commentator said that democratic free speech had been suppressed for too many years. Eleven days later the *People's Daily* said: 'The broad socialist democracy of a proletarian state is based on faith in the masses . . . We believe in you, therefore we grant you democracy.' A week later Teng Hsiao-p'ing was in Washington. He appeared there as the champion of democratic freedom. He was back in China by February 4.

At the end of January there were disturbances in the cities in China, with crowds shouting 'We want democracy!'. On February 21, the special commentator in the *People's Daily*, invoking the authority of Teng Hsiao-p'ing, said that young workers who put up wallposters criticising the Communist Party should not be arrested and or be called counter-revolutionaries, but those who had spread anarchy and disorder should be punished severely. But this time, the Chinese troops were already fighting in Vietnam in what was called a 'self-defensive counter-attack'. Mass demonstrations might have been expected in the cities in support of the war. There were none. On February 5, a day after Teng Hsiao-p'ing's return from the United States, train traffic to Shanghai was halted for twelve hours in protest against the arrest of some youngsters. Democracy had come to an end, and so came

[8] *CNA*, no. 1168, Nov. 23, 1979.

to an end *The Search*, Wei Ching-sheng's short-lived magazine.[9]

The severity of the law was plain for all to see. Death sentences were followed quickly by executions. On August 29, 1979, a court in Canton condemned a man to death for rape and murder; less than a month later, on September 12, the man was executed. On October 9, a county court condemned the son of a minor local official to death for robbery and murder; the sentence was carried out at once. A man who had spent three years in a labour camp killed his accuser on November 6; he was sentenced and executed in the presence of a crowd of some 6,000 on November 19. On February 27, 1980, four young men wounded a bus conductor; one of them was condemned to death and executed on March 24. One of the most famous cases was the condemnation for multiple rape of two sons of the former commander of the Chekiang provincial army, one of Lin Piao's men. A mass meeting was held and one of the young men was given the death sentence which was 'carried out promptly.'[10]

The rule that executions must receive the approval of the Supreme Court was changed by the Legal Commission headed by P'eng Chen in order to speed up the process. Approval by the regional higher courts was to be enough.

In May 1981, when P'eng Chen was still head of the Legal Commission of the Congress, the People's Congress decreed that in the face of growing criminality, the courts should choose the more severe penalty or the 'additional sanction'. It was explained that this meant that the judge should impose, within the range of sanctions laid down in the Criminal Code, the most severe sanction available; 'additional sanction' meant imposing a sanction one grade higher than the maximum prescribed in the Criminal Code. If, for example, the maximum sanction for an offence was fifteen years, the additional sanction would be a life-sentence; if the maximum was a life-sentence, the additional one would be capital punishment.[11]

[9] *CNA*, no. 1153, April 27, 1979.
[10] *Kuang Ming Daily*, Oct. 24, 1979; March 11, 1980; *PD*, Nov. 15 and 30, 1979; Feb. 28, 1980; and March 25, 1980; *Nan-fang Daily* 南方日報, Canton, Sept. 27, 1979; Ssu-ch'uan Radio, Oct. 9, 1979, and Chekiang Radio, Nov. 29, 1979.
[11] *PD*, Aug. 19, 1981.

In consequence, public executions continued. In some places 10,000, in others 50,000 watched the trials and the executions. On July 17, 1981 in T'ienchin a mass meeting was held in the sports stadium and four criminals were executed on the spot. Two of these were young men who had killed a man because of a girl; one was a shop assistant who had committed homicide in anger; and the fourth was a man who, having completed his term in a labour camp, had killed the man responsible for his condemnation. A photograph of the mass trial was published in the local newspaper, and the mayor of T'ienchin, Hu Ch'i-li (Hu Qili), gave a speech. In Peking, on July 18, 1981, 18,000 people watched the execution of five people in the presence of a vice-mayor of the city. Also in Peking, on September 2, 1981, a former student of the Foreign Language Institute was executed. He had stolen a radio and a pair of sun-glasses from a shop and some money from two bookshops, but when he was caught in one of the bookshops, he struck two guards and one of them died from his injuries. At public trials and executions the public applauded to show approval.[12]

Mao's widow and her followers, who had been arrested one month after the death of the Chairman in early October 1976, were brought to trial in December 1980, together with Lin Piao's four leading generals, who had been arrested in mid-September 1971. With them was the seventy-six-year-old Ch'en Po-ta, who had been arrested and condemned to eighteen years' imprisonment in 1970. He died in 1989. They were all accused of having opposed Mao – and Teng Hsiao-p'ing. The trial, which was televised, lasted till January 25. The whole country was able to see the outburst of anger by Chiang Ch'ing, and hear her assertion that in her person Chairman Mao was standing in the dock. The sentences were death with two years' suspension of execution for her and for Chang Ch'un-ch'iao, and a life-sentence for Wang Hung-wen (Wang Hongwen), whom Mao had picked out as his possible successor twelve years earlier when he was only thirty-three. At the age of thirty-eight he had been made a Vice-Chairman of the Communist Party. The others received sentences

---

[12] *CNA*, no. 1215, Sept. 11, 1981.

ranging from sixteen to twenty years. As the years spent in prison since their arrest were counted, Lin Piao's four generals would have finished their terms in 1987–9. Rumour has it that the death sentence imposed on Chiang Ch'ing has been commuted to life imprisonment.* Nothing has been said about the fate of the others, whether dead or alive.

In March 1982 the Standing Committee of the People's Congress – P'eng Chen still headed its Legal Commission – revised some paragraphs of the Criminal Law of 1979, increasing the severity of sentences: more than ten years in prison, life imprisonment or the death penalty for smuggling, speculative gains, abuse of foreign currency, or theft of cultural relics; and life imprisonment or the death penalty for state employees convicted of receiving bribes, with a note indicating that 'state employees' included all who were working in government organs, in the judiciary, in the army or in state enterprises. This new law was to come into effect on April 1, 1982, but it was ruled that until May 1 those who had given themselves up and informed against other offenders would be given less severe sentences.

This piece of legislation erred by its sheer excess. For years afterwards, bribery, illegal speculation, the smuggling of curios and foreign currency speculation went on unhampered.

A month after this legal act, in April 1982, the highest Party authority, the anonymous 'Party Central', published, jointly with the Cabinet, a long document entitled *Decision on Striking at Serious Economic Crimes*: smuggling, corruption and bribery, theft of goods owned by the State, and so on. No consideration was to be given to any man's status; offenders 'will be suspended from their jobs and expelled from the Party no matter how many years they have been in the Party or whether they occupy high or low posts.' It was prescribed that Party committees and governments of provinces and cities, and Party, government and military departments in the central government must send monthly reports on the progress of this work.

Apparently it did not occur to anybody that this was a travesty

---

*The China News Agency, Xinhua, reported her suicide as having taken place May 14, 1991.

of normal judicial procedure. The Party Central and the Cabinet are not legislative bodies, and thus the Party authorities should not give legal orders to the regional governments or to the military. The highest Party organs can of course impose Party sanctions or expel anybody from the Party. This 1982 order of the Party and the government remained a dead letter; indeed it was considered a dead letter even at the time of its promulgation. 'Some are saying', according to one press report, 'that the policy is not clear and not easy to implement . . . . [Such] severity would divert attention from the main task, modernisation, and would have an adverse effect on the policy of opening towards the outside world and reviving the economic inside.'

In Hupei province, Party and government held a conference to discuss the suppression of economic crime. There it was said that 'some leading comrades do not understand what the whole thing is about.' In July the *Kuang Ming Daily* of Peking said that it was difficult to find one's way through the maze of regulations. Many new elements had appeared in the economy without any legal regulations. In several fields there was no law to rely on and there were no regulations to provide support. Non-criminal acts were sometimes treated as criminal, and serious economic crimes as ordinary breaches of discipline.[13]

LEGISLATIVE POWERS

At the end of 1982 an unexpected but momentous event occurred in China. That sleeping beauty, the People's Congress – which in every Communist country is regarded as a mere rubber-stamp – woke up. The prince whose kiss awoke her was the eighty-year-old P'eng Chen, one of the longest-standing leaders of the Party. It was not a kiss of love, but a kiss of anger. In that year at the 12th Party Congress, P'eng Chen had not become a member of the Politburo's Standing Committee, which consisted of the ailing Yeh Chien-ying (Ye Jianying), Li Hsien-nien (Li Xiannien), Ch'en Yün (Chen Yun), Teng Hsiao-p'ing, Hu Yao-pang (Hu Yaobang) and Chao Tzu-yang (Zhao Ziyang), three orthodox-Leninists versus three reformers.

[13] *CNA*, no. 1239, Aug. 13, 1982.

In 1983 P'eng Chen was to take the place of Yeh Chien-ying as head of the National People's Congress, but in preparation for the meeting at which this change-over would become effective, a new Organisation Charter of the People's Congress was published in December 1982. This Charter gave the Standing Committee of the People's Congress the right to promulgate laws, a right which till then had belonged to the National Congress alone; it was decided moreover that its Standing Committee should meet every second month. The Cabinet – State Council – was given no more than the right it had possessed before, to publish Decisions, Decrees and Regulations.

Up till then, the unwritten but strictly observed rule was that before the yearly plenary session of the People's Congress, the Party Central Committee should hold a meeting to prepare the programme for the session. The People's Congress would then express its approval unanimously. However, in December 1982, for the first time, there was no Party meeting before the meeting of the National People's Congress.

There was more to come. At the Party Congress of 1982, Teng Hsiao-p'ing eliminated from the Central Committee some prominent Party and government leaders. When P'eng Chen took over leadership of the People's Congress in 1982, these men whom Teng Hsiao-p'ing had rejected were named deputy heads of the Standing Committee of the People's Congress. The Standing Committee established six sub-committees, and four of them were headed by men who a year earlier had been dismissed by Teng Hsiao-p'ing. P'eng Ch'ung (Peng Chong), who had been dropped from the Politburo, became head of the Legal Commission. Wang Jen-chung (Wang Renzhong), who had won fame by swimming with Mao in the Yangtzu river in 1966, and who had filled various important posts becoming head of the State Agricultural Commission in the 1980s, was among those dropped from the Central Committee Secretariat in 1982, but P'eng Chen took him back and made him head of the Finance and Economic Commission of the People's Congress. Keng Piao was a former Vice-Minister of Foreign Affairs and in 1981 was Minister of Defence; he too lost his job in 1982 but became head of the Foreign Affairs

Commission of the People's Congress. P'eng Chen had gathered round himself in the People's Congress men with distinguished Party careers who had been rejected by Teng Hsiao-p'ing. He thus turned the People's Congress into a rival Party organisation.

P'eng became a major power. Before he became head of the People's Congress, he was head, within the Party, of the Politico-Legal Commission, which controlled the security organs, the police, the courts, the procuratorate and a powerful new body established at the end of 1982: the People's Armed Police. When he became head of the People's Congress, this post was taken over by Ch'en P'i-hsien, another veteran Party leader, who was made first among the deputy heads of the Standing Committee of the People's Congress. His post as head of the Politico-Legal Committee was taken over in 1985 by an up and coming younger man, Ch'iao Shih (Qiao Shi). P'eng Chen remained the power behind him.

In 1984, as the head of the highest legislative body, P'eng Chen said publicly things which in those days would have been interpreted in any Communist country as a revolt against the highest Party authorities. In May 1984 he told journalists that 'the policy of the Party must pass through the state [i.e. the People's Congress] to become the policy of the state.' The policy, he said, must be laid down in the form of legislation. Ch'en P'i-hsien declared that the People's Congress was the highest legislative organ and that the Cabinet, the State Council, was only an executive body.[14] In 1985 P'eng Chen said: 'Naturally the laws are based on the policies of the Party Central, but not all policies will become law immediately.' The building up of a legal system is long and painstaking work. 'It is not something that can be done in three to five years. Today there are many people who have not even studied the Constitution [which had been published three years earlier]. The working process of the People's Congress Standing Committee itself will have to be built up further to enable it to do proper legislative work.'[15]

[14]L. Ladany, *The Communist Party of China and Marxism, 1921–1985*, C. Hurst, London, 1988, pp. 485–6, 457–9, 464, 485–6.
[15]*PD*, Aug. 16, 1985.

The People's Congress and its Standing Committee were busy formulating new laws. It was a slow operation. Seven years passed after the promulgation of the Criminal Code in 1979 until a Civil Code was passed on April 12, 1986 to enter into force on January 1, 1987.

CIVIL LAW

Even then, the new law was not a complete code, but only a collection of general principles. The draft was presented, and its genesis explained, at the People's Congress Standing Committee in November 1985. It was announced that a draft had been prepared before the Cultural Revolution; a draft committee had then been set up in 1979 and the draft rewritten four times by 1982. In those years the economic structure of the country was undergoing great transformations – the People's Communes were dissolved and more free trade was allowed – and it had been difficult to adjust the draft to the changing times.

The socialist economy is based on common ownership, yet by 1985 there were already 10 million private traders. The draft civil law had to guarantee the rights of the individual and of legal persons. For more than three decades China had heard nothing about 'legal persons'. The 1985 draft – the final text – said that if state organs or civil servants infringed the rights of an individual or of a legal person they would have to bear civil responsibility.

The relator, Wang Han-pin (Wang Hanbin), head of the Law Compiling Commission of the Congress, explained that individual civil law acts had already been promulgated. There was a Marriage Law, a Heredity Law, a Patent Law, a Trademark Law, and some laws dealing with foreign business in China.

The Civil Law – General Principles, consisting of nine Chapters, with 156 Articles – was similar to a Western civil code. It dealt with natural and legal persons, and with civil rights and obligations. It regulated rights to inventions and trademarks and established the principle of defending personal reputations. It proclaimed the inviolability of state ownership and 'non-infringement on state economic plans'. It took into account the economic reforms, and defended the rights of individual traders and all that had been introduced since the dissolution of the Communes under the heading 'responsibility system' of individual farmers or farmers' families. It acknowledged the rights of citizens to owner-ship of their 'incomes and of their houses, savings, livestock, trees and production material and other wealth allowed by the law'. All land is owned by the State but is used either by the 'whole people', i.e. by the state directly, or by the collective. The individual citizen has the right to the use of land granted either by 'the whole people' or by the 'collective'. Land may not be sold, rented or mortgaged. Individual citizens have the right to exploit mines (Articles 80, 81).

A few days before the promulgation of the law, some delegates at the People's Congress brought up the question of land owner-ship and proposed that the words 'the common ownership of the labouring masses of the village' should be omitted from the draft, and they were indeed omitted in the final text. The situation is complicated, it was said. What was owned formerly by the 'pro-duction brigade' is now owned by the village, the individual natural village, and what was owned by the 'great brigade' or the commune is now owned by the 'administrative village' or the *hsiang (xiang)*.

At that Congress debate somebody brought up the fact that many hospitals had refused to accept poor people, even emergency cases, who were not able to pay. Important as the humanitarian principle might be, this did not fit in with the General Principles of the Civil Law.[16]

The Civil Law did not remove all obscurity from the question of land ownership. Two months after it had been passed, a Land Management Law was passed, but this did not make things any clearer. It said: 'Land in the cities is owned by the whole people, i.e. by the state', land in the suburbs being owned collectively (Article 6). State land could be used by units of the whole people (i.e. of the state) or by the collective. Both state land and collec-tive land could be used by individuals (Article 7). Collective land

[16] *PD*, April 9, 1986.

is owned by 'farmers of the village collectively' and is managed
by Production Corporatives or the Villagers' Committee (Article
8). Collective land must be registered with the county government (Article 9). Land owned by collectives or by a unit of the
state, and state land used by the collectives, could be managed by
the collectives or by individuals (Article 12). Disputes concerning
ownership or use of land would be decided by the county government. Disputes between individuals about the use of land, about
state land or collective land, would be solved by the *hsiang* or by
the county government. In case of non-execution of the government decision, application could be made to the courts (Article
53). A commentary in the *People's Daily* said that this law settled
all unresolved questions.

A *People's Daily* commentary added to the text of the Civil Law
made a distinction between civil law and economic laws. Civil
law, it said, deals with relations between citizens and between
legal persons, whereas economic laws adjust the relations between
the state and the enterprises and between the enterprises
themselves. It was admitted that this was a distinction which was
not easy to draw.[17]

It was stated at the September 1987 session of the Standing
Committee that since 1979, some thirty legislative acts concerning
the economy had been passed by the Congress and that the Cabinet
had issued more than 300 Regulations. A law on accounting
had been published in January 1985, one on statistical work in
December 1983, one on weights and measures in September
1985, one on land management in June 1986, one on forests in
September 1984, one on mining in March 1986, one on fishing
in January 1986, one on drugs in September 1984, and so on.[18]

On the whole, the People's Congress did a good job. It was
tackling difficult issues, one after another, and it introduced an
entirely new style. Under Mao, indeed until P'eng Chen took over
the leadership, every bill had been passed by the People's Congress
unanimously. Under P'eng Chen, amendments proposed from the
floor were discussed and published in newspapers, and if there was

[17] *PD*, April 17, 1986.
[18] *PD*, Sept. 5, 1987.

not a relative consensus, discussion of the bill would be postponed till the next session of the Standing Committee, which since 1983 has held a session every alternate month. However, the number of votes given for or against a bill has never been announced.

For twenty-two years, 1957–79, China had been a legal jungle. In 1955, at the beginning of the short-lived period of legal vitality, it was announced by P'eng Chen, who in those days was Secretary-General of the People's Congress Standing Committee, that four organs were designated as authoritative interpreters of laws and decrees – the People's Congress and its Standing Committee, the Supreme Court, the Academy of Science for defining scientific terms, and the *People's Daily*. In this respect it was the *People's Daily*, of the four, which turned out to be the most important. Indeed, its editorials expressing the will of the Communist Party often went ahead of the promulgation of laws and decrees.[19]

When, after some twenty years, legal work began anew in June 1981, the People's Congress Standing Committee made a decision on legal interpretation – a very different one from the decision of 1955. The Cabinet or its departments would have the right to interpret laws and decrees concerning them; the Supreme Court and the Supreme Procuratorate would have the same right; but the last word would lie with the Standing Committee of the People's Congress. This decision on legal interpretation added a long paragraph saying that since knowledge of law and legalism in China is extremely defective, it recommended that model cases be formulated to enable the public to learn the rule of law.[20]

Thus the process of legislation was on the march. Many of the legislative acts, however, remained on paper only. There was no way in this highly disciplined Communist country of enforcing the implementation of the laws. A report presented at the 1984 yearly session of the People's Congress said: 'To many people the notion of acting according to the law is new, unfamiliar, not something they are used to.' And in the following years, this

[19] *PD*, July 18, 1985.
[20] *Chung-hua jen-min kung-he-kuo fa-lü chi yu-kuan fa-kuei hui-pien* 中華人民共和國法律及有關法規滙編 (Compilation of Laws and Legal Regulations of the People's Republic of China), Peking, 1986, pp. 425–6.

refrain also appeared many times in the press. In October 1986 the State Economic Commission and the Ministry of Justice declared jointly that over 300 laws and regulations had already been published concerning the economy, but 'their non-observance is quite universal.' This was because the heads of the enterprises had no notion of law; there were no legal experts to advise them; and there was no machinery to control the implementation of laws and regulations.[21]

The same difficulty was found in enforcing court decisions. In July 1986 the *People's Daily* carried an article with the headline 'The Verdicts and Decisions of the Court Must Be Carried Out'. Some units, notably, state organisations, were refusing the verdicts and declaring publicly that they were wrong and void, the article said. Some even resorted to violence in resisting implementation. Article 57 of the Criminal Law states that resisting the execution of court verdicts is punishable by a fine, detention or a maximum of three years in prison. This applied to criminal as well as to civil cases. 'Some organisations say: "The People's Court, like ourselves, is a state organisation guided by the Party. It cannot have special privileges and cannot force its opinion on other government organisations."' The answer was: 'The (1982) Constitution states that a People's Court makes its decisions independently, without interference from administrative organs, social organisations or individual persons.'

'Some say that any organisation or any person may make mistakes and the People's Courts are not exceptions.' This was rebutted by saying that 'in the court one, two or three judges deliberate over the verdict; there is a jury and there is the right of appeal and eventual revision of the verdict at higher courts.' Thus the verdict had a solid basis. And so the arguments went on.[22]

In December 1982, a law on the Protection of Cultural Relics had been published. Five years later the shocking news was published in the official press that great numbers of ancient graves had been dug up and robbed, with their precious contents being

[21] *PD*, Oct. 7, 1986.
[22] *PD*, July 18, 1986.

sold as curios to foreign agents through Hong Kong and Macau. In some regions, which had been important centres under the Han Dynasty two millennia ago, no ancient grave remained intact and bones had been found scattered by the robbers over large areas. Whole villages were engaged in robbing graves. The local authorities did not care, and when a fine was imposed, the delinquent paid promptly. It was only a small fraction of the money he had made.[23]

A Forest Protection Law was enacted in September 1984, but years later the press reported that irreplacable forests were being devastated by tree-felling, which was going ahead unimpeded. The same fate befell the September 1984 law on Management of Drugs, which, in sixty neat articles, regulated the registration of all those engaged in manufacturing and selling medicines. Three years later the press published alarming reports of fake and dangerous drugs being sold freely throughout the country.

The government made praiseworthy efforts to redress the situation and urged the execution of the laws. But the relaxation of the economic system, the erosion of Party discipline and the official encouragement given to people to make money through their own efforts – to which the Party cadres took no exception – made the implementation of the regulations almost impossible. The fundamental difficulty lay in the dissolution of the traditional Chinese moral texture. An example may be found in the attitude towards the deep-rooted conviction that graves are inviolable. Digging up ancient graves had always been considered an act of sacrilege that would call down the wrath of Heaven. It was the People's Republic that broke this rule, excavating great numbers of ancient graves. The findings contributed considerably to knowledge of archaeology and of ancient Chinese history, and attracted large numbers of foreign tourists; but the spell had been broken and unscrupulous agents and local villagers exploited the new situation.

During the thirty years of Mao's rule, the moral texture of the nation was torn to shreds. The younger generation have hardly heard of traditional morality. The endless political campaigns,

[23] PD, July 5 and 8; and Sept. 2, 1987.

campaigns of class hatred, blew through society like a hot sirocco, creating a vast desert.

At the end of 1984 the local *Peking Daily*, the newspaper of Peking city, said that there was wide ignorance of laws and legal matters among the civil servants and even among Party leaders. It was still believed that laws tie the hands of administrators, and indeed Mao had said that law is not indispensable; that Party policy is enough, and Party leaders can decide what is to be done. These people do not understand that laws are necessary to maintain people's democracy, that they create stability.[24]

A great campaign was started to spread knowledge of law and legality. In June 1985 Ch'en P'i-hsien summoned to Peking all heads of Party propaganda and of provincial departments of legal administration to launch a campaign for increased legal knowledge. He said that this should be spread through all channels – schools, newspapers, radio and television. He hoped that within five years the public at large would acquire the main elements of legal knowledge.[25] In the middle of the 1980s seventy-one periodicals were specialising in law. Several of them were popular magazines full of thrilling crime stories; others were serious periodicals, and two of these dealing with the judicial systems of other countries. In November 1985, the Legal Department of the Party Propaganda department held a National Conference of these publications at which the highest State organs – the Law Commission of the People's Congress, the Supreme Court, the Ministry of Security, and so on – were represented.[26]

However, all this propaganda for legality and the provisions of the Criminal Law with all its severity had little effect. Bribery and corruption, the theft of precious objects and other crimes continued unabated, and newspapers were frank enough to report many grave scandals – obviously published to intimidate others.

A formidable list of crimes was reported in 1985: collective corruption in state-owned firms, illegal importation of tens of thousands of cars, government cadres engaging in shady business

[24] *PD*, Dec. 17, 1984.
[25] *PD*, June 15, 1985.
[26] *PD*, Nov. 10, 1985, and May 12, 1986.

and illegally selling old railway wagons, false economic reports, the theft of letters by post-office employees, the existence of fifty illegal companies run by Party members in a single city, 283 fake companies run by local Party leaders in a province (Shensi), selling fake and harmful drugs, forgery of United States and Hong Kong banknotes, forgery of college diplomas, private tailoring and sale of uniforms, the sale of railway tickets on the black market, private selling by state steelworks at high prices (in Wuhan), the sale of fake aluminium with the involvement of twenty Party members. Between January and November 1985, 5,900 major cases of corruption were detected, twice as many as in the previous year; many were collective corruption cases.[27]

A brief summary of cases in 1986: corruption in many provinces involving Party officials, even the judiciary; illegal importation of a large quantity of television sets (four arrested; an ex-minister was punished by the Party); a big swindle at the provincial weather bureau of Kuangsi; abuses of power supply, cutting off power as a means of extortion; illegal sales of steel and of railway wagons; currency speculation in government offices in Kuangtung; senior government officials involved in corruption in Hopei; large-scale thefts in post offices; illegal pocketing of 1,100 million yüan in the finance department of an area in Fukien; and in Peking itself abuses in power supply, departments of the city administration found corrupt, and large-scale corruption in the running of Peking railway station.[28]

In 1987: huge sums allocated to education diverted to other purposes in Kuangtung; black market petrol sold throughout the country; illegal sale of railway tickets at enhanced prices all over the country; fake fertilisers sold to peasants in Hunan and Kansu; collective corruption in Shenyang city; corruption practised by the manager of Taiyüan Steelworks; Party officials selling objects stolen from tombs and museums; the provincial governor of Kuangsi jailed for corruption; fake wine and drugs discovered;

[27] PD, July 22, 1985; Aug. 1, 2, 20, 21, 22, 24; Sept. 1, Oct. 24; Nov. 7, 8, 10, 23; Dec. 23; and Feb. 1, 1986.
[28] PD, Jan. 23; Feb. 7, 22, 26; July 13; Aug. 16, 30; Sept. 2, 3; and Oct. 19 and 25, 1986.

government funds destined for agriculture embezzled.[29] The number of detected economic crimes in 1985–6 rose by 50 per cent.

The cumulative impression that one gains from these reports is that the corruption and breaches of the law were not sporadic individual cases but collective actions by Party leaders. In many cases the grown-up children of officials abused their social status and, using the authority of their parents, made large sums of money under the pretext of engaging in economic reform. A typical example was a trading company established in Ch'angsha, the capital of Hunan province. The board of directors consisted of nine offspring of Party officials. The company existed in name only; it had no funds, no technical personnel, not even offices. The directors engaged in buying and selling textile products, television sets, cars and steel products, and announced the holding of a national exhibition of high-quality products. When the swindle was revealed, their parents, government and Party officials, tried to cover it up; but it became a public scandal and the Party boss of the province, Mao Chih-yung (Mao Zhiyong), had to step in.[30]

This type of corruption was so widespread that in September 1985, when an Extraordinary National Party Conference was being held, the aged Ch'en Yün, a member of the highest governing body, the Standing Committee of the Politburo, and head of the Party's Disciplinary Investigation Committee, made a statement saying that since the end of 1984, 20,000 new companies had been set up, most of them run by inter-related Party cadres and their children. These companies had engaged in business with foreign businessmen, speculative buying and selling, corruption and evasion of customs duties and taxes. The crimes enumerated by Ch'en Yün were endless. These companies, he said, were engaged in selling fake drugs and adulterated alcohol and even in spreading pornographic videotapes and luring women

[29] PD, Feb. 20, 1987; April 7, 20, 25, 27; May 5, 16, 21, 27; June 18, 20; and July 2, 1987.
[30] PD, Sept. 13, 1985.

into prostitution[31] – a genuine Mafia organisation in the Party ranks.

In January 1986, Hu Ch'i-li – whom we met at the public execution in 1981, when he was the Party boss in T'ienchin city – addressed the Central Party School. By this time he was already a member of the Politburo. He spoke of criminal Party members: 'Let those who should be killed be killed! To kill one is a warning to hundreds . . . The higher the rank of the cadre whose child is accused, or of the cadre (if he himself is a criminal), and the more famous he is, the better. It [his execution] will serve as an example.'[32]

In the following month a deputy Party secretary of Shanghai city – who should have had nothing to do with legal cases – declared that the utmost severity of law was to be imposed, and that no children of Party leaders would be spared.[33] Action followed quickly. Six young men, sons of Party cadres, were condemned for multiple rape. Two were given long prison sentences and two were executed. The sensational aspect of this was that the two who were executed were sons of a well-known Party leader.

This, however, was the beginning and the end of the pursuit of the offspring of Party leaders. Rumours circulating in Hong Kong promised the execution of more children of high Party leaders, but nothing happened. Obviously there had been an outcry among high Party officials against such severity. Hu Ch'i-li had disturbed a hornet's nest.

LAWYERS

The courts were poorly equipped to serve the law. The judges had hardly any training and it was still held that 'in accusing a person the state cannot err'. Cases were reported of judges ejecting the defence lawyers from the court. There were regional Party leaders

---

[31] *PD*, Sept. 27, 1985.
[32] *Li-lun yüeh-pao* 理論月刊 (Theory Monthly), Peking, no. 2, 1986.
[33] *PD*, Feb. 20, 1986.

who declared that defence lawyers did not fit into the Chinese system.

At the 1985 People's Congress, a representative said that China really needed 2 million trained lawyers, 1 million judges in the courts and 1 million defence lawyers, but only 3,000 a year were being trained in the schools and 30,000 by correspondence courses. At the beginning of 1988, there were 180,000 people working in the courts. Of these, 40,000 had taken only a short course of training in legal work. Some heads of court, and some heads of prosecution offices also, did not have even a basic knowledge of law. Ignorant but politically reliable demobilised soldiers and retired Party officials were acting as judges and prosecutors, while trained lawyers were being squeezed out of their jobs.

It was understandable in these circumstances that the standard of legal and court work was not high. Cases were reported of defence lawyers being accused of 'covering the crimes' of the accused. The judges themselves had a hard, indeed a dangerous job. In October 1988, the spokesman of the Supreme Court said that in a number of cases judges had been attacked by violent intruders and beaten unconscious or had had their property destroyed. Much violence was committed by village clans dissatisfied with court verdicts.

The judges themselves were not blameless. The President of the Supreme Court himself said that some judges had committed serious crimes; they had embezzled court fees, engaged in such illegal business as the speculative selling of cars, steel products or adulterated liquor, and even engaged in prostitution and rape. He cited examples from three provinces, including that of a county court judge in Kueichou province who had kidnapped and obtained ransoms for two women who had appeared in his court in a divorce case.

A press article described the lot of one lawyer who had started working in 1956, the year when the system of defence lawyers was established. A year later, in 1957, the system changed and he was condemned as a 'rightist'. For twenty-three years, so the article said, 'the tool in his hand was not a collection of laws but a hoe or a spade.' In 1980 defence lawyers were re-established, and he began functioning again. When he defended a case, people raised the cry that 'he was purposely opposing the Communist Party'. The article concluded that to be a defence lawyer was dangerous.[34]

THEORY OF LAW, 1985–1989

With the demise of Mao, the law became respectable once more after thirty years of legal vacuum. In 1979 the Ministry of Justice, which had been abolished in 1959, was re-established. The People's Congress or its Standing Committee, began to publish laws. However, there was no agreement on the nature, the Marxist nature, of law. On June 9–15, 1985, the Party Propaganda Department and the Ministry of Justice discussed at a national conference how to propagate the notion of law among cadres and among the young. In Kiangsi province the notion of law was discussed and an Association for Research on the Basic Theory of Law was established. But there was confusion about the very nature of law.

Is law class law or 'social law'? Nobody denied the Marxist axiom that law is a class law, but it was strongly held by some that law is not class law only, but that some laws apply equally to all. Their arguments were: first, are not laws for the protection of the environment, the regulation of traffic and so on applicable to all? And secondly, it is true that Marx, Engels and Lenin defined law as a tool of the class struggle, but there was no longer an exploiting class in China and therefore that definition no longer retained its validity.

There was also discussion, and disagreement, on the question whether in the final stage of Communism there would still be legal coercion.[35]

For thirty-odd years the Chinese people were divided into People and Non-People, the latter being outcasts, enemies of the

---

[34] *PD*, April 7, 1985, Jan. 16, 1988, May 26, 1989, March 26, 1989, Oct. 24, 1988, p. 4; May 7, 1989, May 12, 1985.
[35] *China Encyclopaedic Yearbook* 中國百科年鑑, Peking-Shanghai, 1986, p. 156; *PD*, July 8, 1985.

people, reactionaries, counter-revolutionaries – in other words, millions of Chinese. Mao Tse-tung used to say that only 5 per cent of the population belonged to these categories, but of course 5 per cent meant tens of millions, those who were the 'landlords, kulaks, counter-revolutionaries, bad elements and rightists' and their descendants. Being a Non-Person was like having a hereditary title. The Non-People were true outcasts: they were under continual surveillance, they got the dirtiest work to do, their children could not go to higher schools; and when they were sick they could not get into a hospital. They had to marry among themselves: few people who were not outcasts were ready to make the sacrifice of marrying them and thus acquiring their status. They were like the untouchables in India or the shunned lepers in the old days. China's history had never before known such untouchables. One of Teng Hsiao-p'ing's greatest achievements was the abolition at the beginning of 1979 of the category of Non-People. According to Teng, there was no longer a counter-revolutionary class in China; there were only counter-revolutionaries, individuals who acted against the regime.

But the doctrine that the law is a tool of the ruling class for the oppression of others persisted; orthodox Communists could not imagine that things could be otherwise, although the 1982 State Constitution had laid down (Article 33) that 'all citizens of the People's Republic of China are equal before the law'. In January 1986, a lawyer wrote: 'In our society there are still some counter-revolutionary elements, enemy spies, criminal elements in the field of the economy and other criminal elements who work for the destruction of social order.'[36] He continued: 'We must firmly hold the Four Basic Principles [Party leadership, Dictatorship, Marxism, Socialism] and must use law as a weapon.' On the other hand, 'We must defend people's democratic interests.' He arrived at the conclusion: 'The class character of the people's democratic dictatorship of our socialist legal system must be upheld in theory and practice.'[37]

---

[36] The term 'elements', as opposed to 'persons', dates from the Mao era.

[37] *Cheng-fa lun-t'an* 政法論壇 (Politico-Legal Tribune), published by the Chinese Politico-Legal University, Peking, no. 1, 1986, p. 29.

The review *Fa-hsüeh* (Jurisprudence) published an article in 1986 about the 'one country two systems' laid down for the future Special Areas of Hong Kong, Macau and eventually Taiwan. 'Taiwan, Hong Kong and Macau are ruled by the exploiting class and therefore their laws are expressions of the bourgeois class. They will all be under the Constitution [of China]. The class character of the Constitution is beyond dispute.'[38]

Chang Hao (Zhang Hao), a professor of theory of law at the Chinese Politico-Legal University, Peking, was a perfect example of a man who could think only in old-fashioned Marxist terms; he finished his legal studies in the same school in 1953. In 1988 he discussed in the journal of the school whether in the final stage of Communism, when the state withers away, there will still be law. Mao had answered this affirmatively, saying that when class struggle is no more, people will still quarrel, and therefore courts and law will be needed, and Chang Hao quoted these words as proof.[39]

A strange article appeared in 1987 in the same quarterly. It sorted the crimes listed in the Criminal Code of 1979 into two categories: crimes of 'enemy-and-us contradiction' and crimes 'within the people'. The distinction is an old one, which had received its classic expression – often reiterated – from Mao three decades earlier, in 1957, in his well-remembered speech on 'Antagonistic Contradictions'. According to that speech there are antagonistic and non-antagonistic contradictions. The non-antagonistic are contradictions 'within the People'. In the days of Mao's reign, counter-revolutionaries, kulaks, reactionaries and bad elements, as they were called, and their descendants belonged to the Non-People.[40] This classification into People and Non-People was suppressed by Teng Hsiao-p'ing, as we saw above, and replaced by the doctrine that there are still counter-revolutionary acts committed by individual persons.

---

[38] *Fa-hsüeh* 法學, Shanghai, no. 5, 1986, p. 13.
[39] Politico-Legal Tribune, no. 22, 1988, p. 15.
[40] Cf. Mao Tse-tung, *On the Correct Handling of Contradictions among the people*, speech made on February 27, 1957, at the 11th Session (enlarged) of the Supreme State Conference, Foreign Languages Press, Peking, 1957.

This 1987 article in the quarterly 'Politico-Legal Tribune' resumed the old Maoist distinction, sorting out criminal cases into antagonistic and within-the-People crimes. It said that all counter-revolutionary acts, listed in the 1979 Criminal Code in Articles 91–102, are crimes of 'enemy-and-us' – as are all other crimes which endanger society. It added a tabulation of seventy articles of the Criminal Code, sorting them into the two categories: the responsibility for major accidents, for instance, falsifying trade-marks, illegal hunting, stealing, cheating and issuing false docu-ments, were listed as crimes within-the-People, whereas habitual stealing and smuggling were 'enemy-and-us' crimes. A number of crimes could be found in one category or the other, according to whether the damage done to society was greater or smaller. Thus forging currency is an 'enemy-and-us' crime if the amount forged is large. So also are torture used in extracting confessions of crimes if heavy injury is inflicted, and corruption of officials if great damage is caused.[41]

This return to Mao's 1957 doctrine – the division of people into People and Non-People – together with its application to the 1979 Criminal Code, was unexpected. It showed that there was a con-siderable malaise, and that deep division among lawyers and between factions in political life was endemic.

The doyen of Party lawyers was Chang Yu-yü, a master of ambiguity. Born in 1899, he studied law in the 1930s, entered the Communist Party in 1927, and filled various distinguished posts such as Party secretary of Peking and head of the Legal Research Institute. In 1986, writing on the occasion of the fifth anniversary of the establishment of the Chinese Society of Politics, he said that for thirty years the study of politics had been non-existent; yet he also insisted that Marxism and Leninism should not be aban-doned.[42] In 1988, in the newly-established Party paper *Ch'iu Shih* (Qiushi; the continuation of 'Red Flag'), he noted with satis-faction that in fifty schools of higher learning 40,000 students were studying law. He inveighed against slavish imitation of the

---

[41] *Politico-Legal Tribune*, no. 4, 1987, pp. 70–4.
[42] *Cheng-chih-hsüeh yen-chiu* 政治學研究 (Political Science Research), Peking, no. 1 1986, p. 3.

Western bourgeois legal system, but also against rigid adherence to the dogmatic legal doctrine of the past.[43] In 1987 he wrote about the People's Congress and its Standing Committee. In these, as in all government organs, the Party organisation should not give direct orders, he said, but it can guide Party members in the People's Congress or in government offices. Chang Yu-yü believes that Western-style separation of powers is out of the question; yet he holds that the heads of courts should not be dismissed on the orders of the Party committee: the Party charter itself says that 'the Party should move within the framework of the State Constitution and of the laws'.

Chang Yu-yü thus tried to solve the insoluble problems of how to maintain the Party policy while creating a sound legal system. The Party committee in every legal organisation, be it the People's Congress or the courts, should dictate from the background but should not interfere directly in legal business, and arbitrary action by a Party leader in the appointment or removal of court officials should be avoided. The line of demarcation between what the Party can and cannot do has not yet been defined, he said.[44]

On the other side, there was a strong trend towards reform. As early as 1980, when Teng Hsiao-p'ing was producing his liberal programme, voices were heard quoting Montesquieu and his separation of power between the legislature, executive and judiary. This was proposed as a guide for the future of China, but Teng himself declared in 1986, at the time of a student demonstration, that in China there would be no separation of power.[45] However, this did not stop the speculation of some liberals. The March 1987 edition of a publication of the Academy of Social Sciences, 'Political Science Research', carried an article arguing that political power originates from the people and the state should do only what individual citizens cannot do. It pointed out that, contrary

---

[43] *Ch'iu Shih* 求是 (Search for truth), Peking, no. 2, 1988, pp. 22–6.
[44] Political Science Research, no. 2, 1987, pp. 1–8.
[45] *PD*, Oct. 30, 1980; *CNA*, no. 1195, Dec. 5, 1980; and Teng Hsiao-p'ing, *Chien-shih yu chung-kuo t'e-sse-te she-hui chu-i* 鄧小平：建設有中國特色的社會主義 (Building of Socialism with Chinese Characteristics), Speeches of Teng Hsiao-p'ing in 1982–7, Hong Kong edn, p. 135.

to this, some contemporary theorists in the Soviet Union were still teaching that political power comes from above.[46]

In January 1986 the review *Fa-hsüeh* launched a discussion on the 'concept of law'. It started with an article by a respected lawyer of the older generation, Chang Tsung-hou (Zhang Zonghou). He recalled that in 1981 he expressed the idea that law is not a product of class struggle, and was accused of teaching anti-Marxist theory. The author now said: 'Most of our teaching material defines law as a manifestation of class will; the teachers follow the definition given by Vyshinski in 1938 in the Soviet Union.[47] Lawyers in our country teach that the origin of this definition goes back to the 1848 *Communist Manifesto*, but this is an error of translation. The Russian text uses two words, "*pravda*" and "*zakon*". Both have several meanings: the *Communist Manifesto* has no definition of law. Our confusion comes from a wrong translation into Chinese.'

A writer in the September 1986 issue of the same review continued the argument on mistranslation, referring not to the Russian translation of the Communist Manifesto but to the original German word '*Recht*'. This term has been wrongly translated, he said. In the decree of the Communist Party of 1949, which abolished all previous legislation in China, it was translated '*fa-ch'üan*' (*fa-quan*), legal power. The same translation was used in the 1970s under the rule of Chiang Ch'ing and her companions, when 'bourgeois rights' were being attacked. After her fall, along with that of the 'Gang of Four', the translation of this term was corrected. Through the years the word '*Recht*' has gone through a variety of translations: '*fa-lü*', law; sometimes '*fa-lü-hsüeh*, science of law; sometimes jurisprudence; sometimes '*ch'üan-li*,' rights. The Chinese term '*fa*' (law), does not distinguish between abstract and concrete concepts of law.

The conclusion was that the *Communist Manifesto* does not give a definition of law in any sense. Be that as it may, could anyone say that a traffic law or a law protecting the environment is class law?[48]

---

[46] *Political Science Research*, no. 3, 1987, p. 46.
[47] Andrei Y. Vyshinski was the harsh public prosecutor under Stalin.
[48] *Fa-hsüeh*, no. 1, 1986, pp. 4–5.

This subtle linguistic discussion seeking to prove that the doctrine of law being taught in China as part of Marxism – that law is class law – comes from a wrong translation of the *Communist Manifesto* could easily be refuted. The 1848 *Manifesto* states clearly: 'Political power is merely the organised power of one class for oppressing another', and the very first words of the Manifesto are: 'The history of hitherto existing society is the history of class struggle.'

The old Marxists still had a dominant voice, and the liberal undercurrent moved cautiously. In May 1988 a conference was held, purposely far from Peking, in Chuhai, close to Hong Kong and Macau. According to the agreements with Britain and Portugal, these places, after their return to China – Hong Kong in 1997 and Macau in 1999 – are to retain their capitalist systems. Chuhai was thus a suitable place in which to air liberal legal theories. In China the norm is public ownership; in the capitalist world it is private ownership. The conference did not take sides but it stated that legal theory had developed in China in the preceding ten years. The legal system, however, was still adhering to the old rigid concepts; there were still many gaps both in legislation and in theory; and the influence of legal theories learnt from Vyshinski during the Stalinist period in the Soviet Union was still strongly felt.

At this conference two young men of the Law Research Institute of the Academy of Social Science argued strongly that the old legal theory of Vyshinski should be rejected. According to this theory, law was a tool of class struggle, and its purpose dictatorship and the suppression of differing views and doctrines. This, the younger men said, was not real Marxism but nonetheless it was still prevalent in leading circles. 'The concept of legality is still very weak among people. The concept of a legal state has not yet penetrated into the ranks of the leaders.'[49]

In January 1989 a particularly heated conference on legal matters was held in Shenchen (Shenzhen), on the Hong Kong border. As reported by a well-known Chinese lawyer, Yu Hao-cheng, in an interview given to a Hong Kong newspaper, the reformists stood

[49] *PD*, Sept. 5, 1988.

up firmly to the Party lawyers. They said that the Preamble of the 1982 State Constitution, which states the Party's Four Basic Principles of Party leadership, Dictatorship, Marxism and Socialism, is only a preamble and has no legal force. They also said that a new constitution should be drawn up, a constitution of China, not of People's China. The Parliament, they said, should have two political parties, the Communist Party and the Kuomintang.[50] One of the leading reformists was Su Shao-chih (Su Shaozhi), who from 1979 till 1987 was head of the Research Institute of Marxism in the Academy of Social Science. In 1987 he was expelled from the Party and after the events of June 4, 1989 he fled from China altogether.

---

[50] *Ming Pao* 明報, Hong Kong, Jan. 22, 1989.

5

LABOUR CAMPS

Not once in the four decades and more since the People's Republic of China was founded has its government published statistics on the number of its prisons it has or prison inmates within them, and no official report has appeared on the system and life inside the prisons. It is known that a few big prisons in major cities are well run. Among these is that old British institution, the Ward Road Prison, now called T'i-lan-ch'iao (Ti-lan-qiao) in Shanghai, and the Number One Model Prison in Peking, which is shown to foreign visitors. It is also known from people who have spent time inside that in many prisons the inmates sleep in crowded cells, packed together like sardines, and that all have to turn from one side to the other simultaneously at the command of a guard. On the whole, except for the years of the Cultural Revolution, there has been no physical torture in the better organised institutions, but prisoners have been told that if they induce cellmates to confess their crimes they themselves may win 'merits' and be released earlier than they would otherwise. This has led to much violence in prison cells. The Communist press itself has described, and blamed, local Party officials who have set up illegal prisons and tortured people. It is known that during political purges people have been locked up for months for questioning, their families knowing nothing of their whereabouts. Sometimes at the end of their psychological torture, they were released with only a word of apology.

Little, as we have said, has been revealed about the number of prisons in the People's Republic or about conditions within them. More has been said about labour camps.

A book, 'The History of Chinese Prisons', published in Peking in 1986, traces the subject from the dawn of Chinese history up till 1949, when the People's Republic was established. The last part of the book deals with the system in the Communist-occupied areas during the civil war. In July 1937 a Higher Court was established in the Yenan area with a detention centre under it. In April 1939 the court ordered that those detained – and not those detained in Yenan only – should take part in productive labour, and the book mentions a labour camp 15 km. from Yenan. In 1941 a special organisation was set up for 'corrective labour': here the inmates were employed in clearing land for cultivation or working in simple factories. But when the Communists began to occupy the cities at the end of 1948, the prisons were not big enough to hold all those arrested, so the prisoners were sent to work in the fields and in mines. They were not welcome, the book says, in the places to which they were sent.

The court in Harbin decided to set up special corrective labour camps, farms and mines, and in these the inmates were organised in military style. Of this the book says: 'The establishment of corrective labour troops began a new chapter in the history of penitentiaries, and they became an important part of the economy. When the whole country was taken over and the suppression of counter-revolutionaries campaign had ended, a great number of counter-revolutionaries were sent to the border areas and to mines. This helped to correct the criminals and to increase production.'[1]

CORRECTIVE LABOUR

The system had been established firmly when its first Regulation, the 'Regulation on Corrective Labour in the People's Republic of China', was published five years later, in August 1954, accompanied by a report by Lo Jui-ch'ing, Minister of Security. The institution of labour camps was learned from the Soviet Union, the minister said. 'During the past four years many agrarian labour reform camps have been established, some of them very large agricultural units, each covering over 10,000 *mou* (667 ha.) of land, and there are also very numerous industrial production units. [. . .] Many labour brigades', he went on, 'have been set to work on water regulation, railway construction, exploitation

[1] Hsüeh Mei-ch'ing and others (eds), *Chung-kuo chien-lao shih* 薛梅卿主編：中國監獄史 (History of Chinese Prisons), members of the Editorial Board of the Corrective Labour Material, Peking, 1986, 384 pp. (45,000 copies printed).

of forests and house-building. They have saved the state huge sums of money and have created a certain amount of material wealth.' In 1953 they produced, among other things, 2,000 million bricks and 700 million tiles. The Peking Textile Factory, also a labour camp, produced 710,000 dozen pairs of socks. Other factories, mines and farms also produced well.

The 1954 Regulation distinguished various kinds of incarceration: detention for those whose cases were pending and for those condemned to terms of less than two years; prison for those condemned to capital punishment with suspension of execution and for those who 'cannot conveniently be sent to work outside the prison'; Corrective Labour (the labour camps); and Juvenile Correction Camps for youngsters aged from thirteen to sixteen.

The Regulation laid down rules for inmates of labour camps; 8–12 hours of work daily, a minimum of an hour of indoctrination; two rest days per month. Relations might come on visits twice a month. Those behaving well and showing readiness to denounce other prisoners might get rewards or be released on parole. The recalcitrants, on the other hand, could have their prison terms extended.

The labour camps – some covered almost a whole county – were well organised. Casual observers would hardly have noticed that the farms or factories they were seeing formed parts of a forced-labour institution. The difference between ordinary farms and factories and these institutions was, as the September 7, 1954 *People's Daily* editorial said, that 'labour was compulsory, unpaid and subject to strict control'.[2]

Once a suspect had been arrested, a plea of not guilty counted as an aggravating circumstance: the government could not err. Detention without trial often lasted for years. The present author had personal knowledge of a man who, having been arrested in 1954, was kept in detention under abominable conditions until 1964, when he was brought to court and sent to a labour camp. The Catholic Bishop of Canton was arrested in 1958 and kept

[2] *CNA*, nos. 53, Sept. 24, 1954; and 56, Oct. 15, 1954; and *Compilation of Selected Laws and Regulations on Security of the Chinese People's Republic* 中華人民共和國公安法規選編, 1982, pp. 195–206.

in prison till 1980. He was never brought to court and never sentenced.

The 1954 Regulation stated that those who had finished their prison or labour camp terms were to be kept in the same locality and work there as 'free' workers, receiving a salary and being allowed to go on visits to their relations once a year. Or they might be sent to settle down in uninhabitated border regions, in which case they were allowed to bring their families to join them – which meant that they would have to stay there for life.[3]

When the Regulation on Corrective Labour was published in September 1954, the International Confederation of Free Trade Unions sent to the United Nations a report based on the documents released by Peking. On December 14, 1954 the United Nations passed a motion condemning forced labour. Peking was highly irritated. The Chinese press complained that it was an insult to call the Chinese corrective labour 'forced labour', just as it had been an insult when the United Nations in 1947 proposed an investigation into forced labour in the Soviet Union. Corrective labour meant teaching people to develop the habit of labour, the press said. There was no forced labour in China, but it did exist in the United States, where workers were jobless, starving and exploited, and university graduates were forced to work as cooks and baby-minders. It was conviently forgotten that the Regulation on Corrective Labour itself used the terms 'corrective labour' and 'forced labour' indiscriminately.

Peking described 'corrective labour' in rosy terms. 'Many inmates continue their confessions of crimes, begun during their trials, and reveal facts which are valuable for the prosecution of other persons.' Indeed the situation was so wonderful that 'on the expiration of their sentences a great number of camp inmates ask permission to remain in the camps.'[4]

Protests from abroad had one result: from then on, the Chinese press rarely used the term 'forced labour'.

[3] CNA, no. 56, Oct. 15, 1954; and Compilation of Selected Laws and Regulations on Security of the People's Republic of China, pp. 207–8.
[4] PD, Nov. 30, 1954; Ta Kung Pao 大公報, T'ienchin, Dec. 17, 1954; also in CNA, no. 70, Feb. 4, 1955.

LABOUR EDUCATION

In 1957 another type of forced labour appeared. In the spring of that year, Mao urged educated people to express their views on how the Communist Party was running the country. They did so, and Mao promptly clamped down, calling them 'rightists' and 'bourgeois', and sent many of them to a new type of labour camp, known as Labour Education.

The official title of the Decision, signed by Chou En-lai, sounded innocuous: Decision on the Problem of Labour Education. But the text said: 'Labour education training is one form of implementing forced educational reform.' Four categories of people were to be sent to this new type of labour camp. First, there were those who broke police regulations and vagabonds who had committed minor thefts or frauds which did not amount to criminal offences – however, there was no legal text in force defining what types of theft and fraud constituted criminal offences. Secondly, there were counter-revolutionaries whose acts did not amount to criminal offences; then thirdly, those who refused to work for a long period or committed breaches of discipline, and finally, people who habitually refused labour assignments or made complaints without good reason. The Decision did not say that it was directed against the 'rightists'; 'those who complained without reason' was enough.

Corrective labour was imposed, by the court – at least in theory. This was not the case with labour education. To this type of labour camp, dating from 1957, 'the government committee of a province or any organ to which this power has been delegated condemns a person on application from any government organ, social organisation, economic enterprise or school or even the head of a family.' The Decision betrayed some vestiges of a desire to legitimise the building of such camps. The text referred to Article 100 of the 1954 Constitution, which said: 'The citizens of the People's Republic of China must abide by the Constitution and the law, uphold discipline at work, keep public order and respect social ethics.'

The whole affair was a travesty of justice. It meant that government organs, not the courts, could send people to forced labour. In fact, those sent to corrective labour and those sent to labour education lived and worked in the same camps.[5]

People were condemned and sent to labour camps on the flimsiest charges. In 1979, three years after Mao's death, the following candid admission appeared in the press: 'A few erroneous words were construed as anti-Party, anti-Socialism; friends who had discussed things among themselves were regarded as an anti-Party clique; the expression of criticism of any leading comrade was taken as an attack on Mao and the central leadership. Such were the grounds for branding a person as "rightist".' The middle class and the more highly educated were the worst hit. Many Party members also were condemned.

At the end of 1959, 142 'rightists' were rehabilitated, including the famous sociologist Fei Hsiao-t'ung (Fei Xiaotong). The majority – their number must have amounted to millions – were not released till 1979, twenty-two years after their condemnation, and even then it was declared that this was not rehabilitation, but merely a correction of erroneous acts. 'The validity of the 1957 anti-rightist struggle cannot be denied. Those people wanted to overthrow the Communist Party and Socialism. We counterattacked in time. This was necessary and correct.' In January 1979, sixty out of the sixty-three 'rightists' in the Ministry of Security were declared to have been wrongly condemned. The other three remained 'rightists'. In the same way, thirty-nine of the ninety-eight former members of the Central Committee Party School were declared to have been wrongly condemned. The other forty-nine remained 'rightists'.[6]

Five years later, at the end of 1984, the process of releasing the 'rightists' had not yet ended. In that year 980 were released; by then many of them were dead.[7]

The labour camp, designed to create the New Man through labour, became a permanent institution. A man who, just before the Cultural Revolution, had scribbled 'Beat down Liu Shao-ch'i' on the margin of a newspaper was sentenced .to forced labour.

[5] *CNA*, nos. 742, Jan. 31, 1969; and 194, Aug. 23, 1957.
[6] *PD*, Dec. 5, 1959; *CNA*, nos. 397, Nov. 16, 1961, and 1152, April 13, 1979.
[7] *PD*, Nov. 2, 1984.

Soon after this, Liu fell, but the man was not released.[8]

In the 1950s a single word spoken against the Russians could send a man to labour camp; in the 1960s a good word for the Russians would have the same effect; yet the man of the 1950s was not released. At the end of the 1960s a word against Lin Piao could be fatal. After the fall of Lin Piao in 1971, a good word for the late Marshal could be fatal. In China now there is no dishonour in having spent years in prison. During the Cultural Revolution men in important positions in the Party, the army and the security organs were arrested and condemned to forced labour. When the political wind changed, they were reinstated in their responsible positions. Many of the elderly Party leaders who occupied in top positions in Peking in the 1980s spent years in labour camps during the Cultural Revolution or were relegated to obscure quarters of the country where they worked in factories. Teng Hsiao-p'ing was only one of these.

This had some unexpected results. During the Cultural Revolution old inmates who had already spent years in labour camps were joined by provincial Party leaders, heads of the provincial security and other people of some importance. The old inmates helped the newcomers to adjust themselves to camp life. When the Cultural Revolution was over and the Party men had regained their former high positions, these hitherto obscure people found after their release that they now had powerful friends among the Party leaders. There was a curious case of a Christian sent to forced labour on account of his faith. A Party man was condemned to the same labour camp. In his desperation he thought of committing suicide, but the Christian taught him the elements of faith and dissuaded him from taking his life. Years later when both had been released, the Christian found a powerful protector in the man whose life he had saved, who was now reinstated in his leading Party job.

Before the Cultural Revolution the Party leaders were not much concerned when the 'enemies of the regime' were sent to forced labour. When, however, they themselves were arrested

[8] *CNA*, no. 1145, Jan. 5, 1979.

and sent to the camps during the Cultural Revolution, they had time to think about the system. After the rise of Teng Hsiao-p'ing at the end of 1978, one of the great reforms was the abolition of the titles 'landlords, kulaks, counter-revolutionaries and bad elements'. The labour camps, however, were not abolished.

CAMPS IN THE TENG ERA

After Teng Hsiao-p'ing had taken over the reins, one of the first legislative acts was the Criminal Code of July 1979. Article 32 of the Criminal Code said: 'When the crime committed is light, not deserving criminal sanction, an admonition may be given, or the offender may be called to express repentance, to apologise, and to repair the damage done. The authorities concerned may impose administrative measures.' What the 'administrative measures' were the Code did not say.

In November 1979, four months after the promulgation of the Criminal Code, the People's Congress decreed that all laws promulgated since the establishment of the People's Republic in October 1949 remained valid, except those not in conformity with the recent legislation. A Supplementary Regulation on Labour Education was published.

A letter to the editor of the *Workers Daily* in Peking asked whether the 1957 Regulation on Labour Education was still valid after the promulgation of the Criminal Code. The reply was 'Yes', referring to the ruling that all laws and decrees of the past remain valid, including the 1951 Regulation on Suppression of Counter-revolutionaries and the 1954 Regulation on Corrective Labour as well as the 1957 Regulation on Labour Education.

The Supplementary Regulation of 1979 decreed that Labour Education Administrations should be re-established in every province and in all major cities. They were to be composed of members of the internal affairs, security and labour departments. The present Administration would decide who should be sent to labour education camps. The term was one to three years, expandable to a fourth year. In the same month a Cabinet Circular repeated what had been said in 1957, that anybody whose actions are 'suspicious' but do not constitute a crime may be sent to a labour camp or to a detention centre while the case is being investigated. It added that 'those in camps or detention centres are to be treated in the same way as those subjected to "forced labour"' (using the term 'forced labour'). The actual running of the camps was entrusted to the security organs.[9]

In June 1981 the People's Congress Standing Committee published a new Regulation. Inmates of labour education camps who escaped were to get longer terms in the camps. Those who had committed crimes within five years of their escape and those who had committed crimes within three years from completion of their terms in the camp were to receive severe penalties. After completion of their new terms, they were to be kept at work in the camp, were not to be allowed to return to visit their families in the cities, and were to lose their residence permits in the cities.[10]

In the early days the inmates of the camps were ex-members of the Nationalist Government, and people considered counter-revolutionary; after 1957 these were joined by the 'rightists'. In the 1980s the character of the camp population changed. Many new arrivals came from proletarian families. Many too were Party members' children, who, taking advantage of the more relaxed political atmosphere and protected by their privileged fathers, had committed crimes of robbery, rape and so on. There were also idealistic youngsters who, like the well-known Wei Ching-sheng, had dreamed of a democratic free society. In 1981, Hsü Chia-t'un, then the First Party Secretary of Kiangsu province, noticed during an inspection tour of his province that 'great changes had taken place in the labour reform and labour education camps. There were great numbers of young people from families of labouring people.'[11] In September 1983, *Red Flag*, the organ of the Central Committee, spoke of this new type of inmate in the camps. 'In

[9] *PD*, Nov. 30, 1979; *CNA*, no. 1180, May 9, 1980; and *Compilation of Selected Laws and Regulations on Security of the People's Republic of China*, pp. 209–12.
[10] *PD*, June 11, 1981; *CNA*, no. 1215, Sept. 11, 1981.
[11] *Hsin-hua wen-chai* 新華文摘 (Hsinhua Digest), Peking, Nov. 9, 1981; *CNA*, no. 1232, May 7, 1982.

our socialist country there is no longer exploitation, but within certain limits class struggle still exists,' it said. 'There are comrades who wonder how it is that many criminals are workers, students, cadres and children of cadres. Many are young. They are not like the camp inmates of the old days, bandits, evil tyrants, political agents.'[12]

The administration in camps came under the Minister of Security. In theory forced labour was meant, through incessant indoctrination, to create the New Man. The reality was very different – with bloody public accusation meetings at which people were beaten and tortured until they collapsed, and nobody dared to come to their defence; murders of accusers by vengeful inmates; weeks and months spent with hands tied, eating on all fours like animals; killing of one inmate by another in the scramble for the last grain of rice, which was doled out to the inmates in buckets as if to animals; heavy labour, which actually crippled many of those subjected to it. Not all the camps and not all the guards were so cruel. In some camps containing tens of thousands of people, there were shops, dispensaries with prisoner-doctors, and theatre troupes. Nevertheless a camp was always a camp. Some inmates were ready to confess to crimes they had never committed. Many accused fellow-inmates in order to receive better treatment; others refused to confess – few of these last left the camps alive.

There are no signs that China, like the Soviet Union, locks up dissidents in mental hospitals. Yet why is the Ministry of Security running sixteen mental hospitals, as was admitted in 1987? Why cannot ordinary hospitals receive the patients? A mental health conference reported in 1986 that there are 348 mental hospitals in China, but it was the Ministry of Security that reported that there are as many as one million mentally ill persons in China who represent a public danger and who are liable to commit crimes such as, murder, arson, rape. The sixteen mental hospitals have a total of only 4,000 beds. The Ministry of Security has asked the provinces to set up

[12]*Hung-ch'i* 紅旗 (Red Flag), no. 17, Peking, 1983, p. 6.

more mental hospitals.[13]

It took the authorities a long time to realise that the way in which the camps were administered was indefensible. In 1984 the administration of the camps was supposed to be taken over from the Ministry of Security by the Ministry of Justice.[14] In the same year an article in the review *Fa-hsüeh* described the treatment of prisoners in labour camps throughout the country. The use of labour camps had begun with the suppression of counter-revolutionaries right after the establishment of the People's Republic in the early 1950s; but the only legal foundation for this institution was the 1954 Regulation. Originally the professed aim of the labour camps was mental reform by productive labour; but this was quickly forgotten. It was time, the article said, for a re-examination of the camps, and the establishment of a Central Law College specialising in labour reform. At the end of 1986 the same review recommended study of the systems used in foreign countries and the introduction of legislation to prevent the arbitrary handling of prisoners. Parole should be granted, not by the armed police of the camps, but by the courts or by a special committee to be set up in the Ministry of Justice. Another law review proposed that the labour camps should not come under the Ministry of Justice, much less under the Ministry of Security, but under a special government organ of the Cabinet. This should have the power to investigate conditions in the camps. Parole and the reduction of prison terms should be decided by the procuratorate and carried out by the administrators of the camps. At present, it said, there are two authorities in the camps, the armed police and the camp administrators, and the two are often in conflict.[15]

In December 1988 a seven-day conference discussed the labour camps. Ts'ai Ch'eng (Cai Cheng), Minister of Justice, explained two things. One was that the existence of labour camps had no

---

[13] *PD*, Oct. 18, 1986, p. 3; Dec. 11, 1987, p. 4; *Wen Hui Pao* 文滙報, Hong Kong, June 1, 1988.

[14] *PD*, April 16, 1985, p. 2.

[15] *Fa-hsüeh*, no. 6, 1985, pp. 12–13; no. 12, 1986, pp. 37–18; *Fa-hsüeh yen-chiu* 法學研究 (Studies in Law), Peking, no. 2, 1987, pp. 66–8.

legal foundations, and that laws should therefore be drawn up to legalise the camps. This was a clear admission that for forty years forced labour camps had been ruled by arbitrary directives from the Party and the Security. The other matter dealt with by the Minister was the modernisation of the camps. Some modern electronic equipment was to be introduced and modern psychological and educational methods learned. The introduction of these new methods, the minister said, might take ten or more years. The main thing, he went on, was to stop the inmates from escaping.

This last statement shows how times have changed. Under the Mao regime people who ran away were infallibly recaptured. The whole country was kept under strict control; people were bound to their own domiciles, and peasants were not allowed to move without special permits. A new face appearing anywhere was easily detected. With the modernisation of the country in the 1980s, millions moved to the cities and towns selling their products or setting up small shops and workshops. It was difficult to keep this mobile population under police control, and those who escaped from the camps could easily hide or take up some occupation in another place without detection.

A remarkable point in the minister's account was that he did not speak of the distinction between inmates who were sent to the camps by the courts for 'corrective labour' and those who were sent by simple administrative measures to 'labour education'. This anomaly – the fact that one's Party boss may send one to forced labour – was to continue.

Although the camps were put under the care of the Minister of Justice in 1984, the minister had only limited power. In the list of the participants at the conference which discussed the labour camps, his name came last. Premier Li P'eng (Li Peng); Ch'iao Shih, member of the Politburo Standing Committee and supreme ruler of the police, courts and labour camps; Wang Feng, minister of Security; and the heads of the Supreme Court and the Supreme Procuration were all listed before him.[16]

The Ministry of Justice was in fact in an awkward position.

[16] *PD*, Dec. 11 and 13, 1988.

A deputy head of the office in the ministry that deals with the labour camps explained this in February 1989 at a conference of lawyers convoked by the review 'Studies in Law'. He said that four organisations deal with the camps, the Security, the Prosecution, the courts and his ministry. No legal acts define the limits of the competence of the four. There are some unpublished internal regulations, but their implementation meets many obstacles. For example, decisions on reduction of an inmate's term in camp or on parole may be issued, but the labour camp authorities, the Security men in the camps, act as they wish.[17]

One would like to know the number of camps and the number of inmates. At a conference on labour camps at the end of 1988, Li P'eng praised the 300,000 policemen working in labour camps. Does this 300,000 give any clue to the number of inmates? If one policeman guards ten inmates, the number is 3 million; if twenty, it is 6 million. According to a deputy minister of justice, schools are run in 473 camps, spread over eighteen provinces.[18] These facts do not indicate either that the other four provinces and eight equivalent areas, five autonomous regions and three cities, embracing 248 counties, have no labour camps.

Hongda Harry Wu (Wu Hung-ta), former inmate of a labour camp who subsequently carried out research at the Hoover Institution at Stanford University, has been able to identify and locate on the map more than 800 labour camps. A report delivered by Cheng T'ien-hsien, head of the Supreme People's Court, which contains the figure of 1,397,000 people sentenced in the twenty-eight months between August 1983 and December 1985, caused Wu to conclude that approximately 600,000 persons are sent to labour camps each year. Wu estimated that, at the time of his research, there were 5–6 million people in labour camps and that altogether there had been 23,400,000 people in them since 1949.[19] The latter figure, particularly, appears much too

---

[17] *Fa-hsüeh yen-chiu*, no. 2, 1989., pp. 23–4.

[18] *PD*, Dec. 11, 1988.

[19] Hongda Harry Wu, 'The Labor Reform Camp in the People's Republic of China', paper presented at the 18th Sino-American Conference, June 8–11, 1989, Hoover Institution, Stanford.

low to the contributors to this book. However, as so often in questions involving quantitative aspects of the socio-political reality of China, one may at least assume that the total number of inmates in labour camps since 1949 has not been less than the figure given.

CAMPS AND ECONOMIC CONSTRUCTION

Forced labour, learned from the Soviet Union, has played a major part in the economic construction of the country. This did not change with the introduction of liberal policies and economic reforms by Teng Hsiao-p'ing in 1979. Indeed, at the December 1988 conference on corrective labour and labour education, Premier Li P'eng emphasised this aspect of the labour camps. 'The Party Central has always paid very special attention to the work of corrective labour and labour education. Without these, socialist construction could not have been guaranteed.'

Forced labour had been applied, for instance,

— in the Huai River water power project which took one million prisoners from Shanghai, Anhui, Kiangsu, Chekiang, Hupei and Shangtung ten years to complete;
— in the reclamation of 2,500,000 *mou* of saline soil in Northern Kiangsu, where 200,000 prisoners from Shanghai and Kiangsu established more than ten state-operated farms;
— in land reclamation in the Pei-ta-huang region in Heilung-kiang by 500,000 prisoners from Peking and from the north-east (Tung-pei);
— in the An-Shan Cooperative Steel and Iron Project and the Pao-Tou Steel and Iron Project, where tens of thousands of prisoners were involved; and
— in Sinkiang and Ch'inghai, where innumerable prisoners have been placed during the past four decades and more. Both regions are China's 'Siberia', synonyms of *katorga*.

Forced labour does not necessarily mean closed camps. Even some important heavy industry plants work with forced labour. A classic example is a plant at Lai-yang city, in the eastern corner

of Shantung province, where 3,700 prisoners, some of whom
are well educated, run an industrial complex producing special
steel products which are sold to Hong Kong, South-east Asia,
the Middle East, Europe and the United States.[20] Many foreign
buyers must have visited the industrial plant, but few can have
grasped the fact that it was a labour camp. Other examples are
the Lin-Fen Automobile Factory in Shensi; the Liang-hsiang
Elevator Factory in Peking; the Hua-tung Electric Welder Plant
and the Lao-tung Glass Plant in Shanghai; the Kuangchou Electric
Fan Factory in Canton; the Peng-p'u Rubber Plant in Anhui;
the Yin-yin Coal Mine in Shensi; the A-erh-t'ai Gold Mine in
Sinkiang; the Chao-yang Lead Plant in Kueichou; the Ch'engtu
Machine Tool Factory in Ssu-ch'uan; the Ying-te Tea Farm in
Kuangtung and the Ch'ing-he Farm in Peking.[21]

All prisons, camps and enterprises attached to the forced labour
system are funded precisely through forced labour. Under the
'System of Contractual Responsibilities in Discipline and Production' which was introduced in the summer of 1984 to make the
economy 'more efficient', 'to make up deficits', and 'to increase
surpluses', inmates and security personnel share responsibility for
the expansion and improvement of production. Under this system
prisoners and police cadres may even become co-managers in a
joint venture, as in the case of the newly-appointed prison commissioner, a certain Mr. Fu, of the Chiang-chen Prison in Wuhu/
Anhui and a long-term prisoner called Shih Cheng which was
reported by 'Democracy and Legal System' in September 1987.

According to this report the prisoner had offered to make
use of his former influence in society so that the prison would
be supplied with steel and could get into a profitable business
by producing nails. That was in 1984. Commissioner Fu took
the prisoner out of detention and, with the approval of the
Party Commission for the prison, established the 'Yangtzu River
Trade Company' in which he made himself the manager and
Shih assistant manager. For this Fu invented the slogan 'Using

---

[20] PD, July 21, 1989.
[21] For this and all further information in this paragraph cf. note 19.

a labourer as a cadre'.[22] Shih was given the company seal, a valid identity card and 220,000 yüan to start the business. In the course of their attempt to make quick money Fu and Shih purchased US $2 million in currency, but a Party decision was passed down decreeing that the purchase of foreign currency was illegal. This ruined their plans. Furthermore, Shih had spent 30,000 yüan on bribes and, while in Canton to contact businessmen from Hong Kong, Shih spent 500,000 yüan on eating, drinking and girls. Eventually a policeman called Hu was sent after Shih. However, Shih was still carrying the $2 million. Somehow he managed to obtain Hu's uniform and police pistol and travelled, wearing them, to T'ienchin and Peking. The prisoner-labourer who had been used as a cadre thus turned into a policeman.

After four months Shih was turned back into a prisoner and was given an addition of twelve years to his sentence. Policeman Hu was disciplined, and Commissioner Fu made his will and committed suicide.

Other cases under the 'System of Contractual Responsibilities in Discipline and Production' have functioned more profitably than this one.

LIFE IN THE LABOUR CAMPS

One searches in vain for a description by the Chinese authorities of what life is like in the labour camps. Still less is there any hope of getting official statistics concerning murders, suicides and other casualties in the camps. Some books have been published abroad by ex-prisoners, but these, though important documents, rarely offer a complete picture. They illustrate the human deprivation suffered in the camps, but they often turn out to be descriptions of the almost incredibly heroic resistance of the writer when in the camp.[23]

[22] As a mutation of the Communist Party slogan 'Using a worker as a cadre'.

[23] *Editor's note.* It is not clear to which reports Father Ladany refers at this particular point. Major descriptions of life in imprisonment in China include Dries van Coillie, *De enthousiaste zelfmoord*, Uitgeverij De Vlijt, Antwerp, and Uigeverij Gesto, Alkmaar, no year given (German edn, Donauwörth 1961); Ruo-Wang Bao, (Jean Pasqualini) and Rudolph Chelminski, *Prisoner of Mao*, New York: Coward, MacCann, and Geoghegan, 1973; Mary Ann Harbert, *Capitivity: 44 Months in Red China*, Michael Joseph, London,

What is given here is a comprehensive image of life in the camps, collected from the testimonies of individuals we have met in the course of more than thirty years, some of whom spent years in labour camps. They may have been working in mines, digging canals, or working either in factories or in the fields, some near big cities and some in the remotest, most sparsely inhabited areas of China. Their working conditions varied greatly; but the regime, the treatment they received, was astoundingly similar, whatever the period or the place. The regulations, the system, dictated by the central authorities, were always the same.

Life in a labour camp was better than life in prison, and prison was better than a detention centre. In detention, murderers were herded together with political dissidents and life was chaotic. Detention is meant to be a transitional stage; but some ex-prisoners have said that they spent many years in detention. Life in prison was better regulated, but it was hard and monotonous. Prisoners might spend years in solitary confinement, which drove many mad, or in overcrowded cells, where they slept on long planks packed so closely together that it was impossible even to turn over. From time to time the benevolent guard shouted: 'Turn', and all would turn together. Everything was done collectively, except the interrogations, which might come daily, or might be delayed, leaving the prisoner in anxious uncertainty for months and sometimes for years.

One day you would be called, packed into a train or truck and sent off on a journey taking you to an uncertain destination. Often the latter part of the journey would consist of several days of marching. You were then in a new environment. You might see a familiar face, but you did not dare to show any sign of recognition; you did not know whether or not he had been 'converted' and become an informer. Even if he had not, the guards might suspect that you would form an inner clique in the prison, something regarded as highly dangerous.

1974; K'e-wen Tuan, *The story of a war criminal*, in *Shih-chieh jih-pao* (The World Daily), Hong Kong, Oct., 1976; and Nien Cheng, *Life and Death in Shanghai*, Grafton Books, London, 1986. It is not suggested that these reports can only be relied on to a limited degree.

In prison or camp your personality would be lost; you became a number, and were known by that number and by nothing else. Throughout the rest of your life you would remember your number in the camp, that you were No. 576 in Team 7, Group 5. There you were not in any way what you had been in the outside world. You no longer had a life of your own; you were a member of the team you worked in; a cog in a machine, getting up at the same time in the morning, marching to work together, doing together the work assigned by the guard, eating together, attending boring indoctrination classes together, exhausted by the daily work. In the evening, you were so totally exhausted that you could not even dream of your family at home. You had ceased to exist.

One thing absorbed all your attention: food. Food in the camps was sufficient for survival, but not sufficient to fill the stomach – light rice porridge, consisting of more water than rice, in the morning, and vegetables, often spoilt, at noon and for supper. You inevitably dreamed of well-cooked, tasty food. What you got had no taste. In many camps for years the staple food was sweet potato. Eaten occasionally, sweet potato is good food; eaten day after day, with nothing else available, it is deadly. Food was served as if to animals. Individual bowls might be filled by the attendants; but a Shanghai lady, who now lives in Paris, recalls how food was put out in buckets and the famished inmates dashed to the buckets like pigs, pushing each other, fighting for the last grain of rice, and ready, as sometimes happened, to kill each other for it. The worst-off were those who had had their arms tied together behind their backs, a not infrequent form of punishment for minor breaches of prison or camp discipline. These unfortunate people literally had to eat like animals, kneeling and bending, unless some kind-hearted cellmate was ready to feed them. The handcuffs, arms twisted back, were not taken off for other functions either, and they had to rely on their cellmates for help.

There was, of course, no choice of work. The team had to reach the working target. The camps were constituent parts of the nation's economy in industry or agriculture. Millions were sent to work in coal mines under primitive conditions, or to dig canals. When landslides buried internees alive, the work went on; no one had time to do anything about them. You were often exposed to danger, but the work could never be interrupted.

On the whole, the camps, particularly the large ones where tens of thousands worked, were well organised. There were small hospitals where prisoner medical staff looked after the sick; often these were ready to order sick-leave for fellow-inmates. These hospitals had little medical equipment and few medicines, but the short rest and the human touch were a great relief. In such mammoth camps theatre groups were organised to entertain camp inhabitants and visiting officials on special occasions.

Occasionally visiting relatives from far-away provinces were allowed in, but they could never meet an inmate alone. A visitor might travel days to meet a son or a husband for half-an-hour. Correspondence was strictly controlled and all letters were read first by the guards. It was up to them to decide whether the letter should be given to the addressee; if it was, the recipient would be interrogated about the contents. Bad news from home, news about sickness or misery in the family, was handed over reluctantly for fear that it would upset the inmate and make him slack in doing his daily work.

Forced labour in China was designed as a psychological laboratory, to produce the New Man by labour and discipline. This idea, imported from the Soviet Union, was as unsuccessful in China as in Russia. The Chinese, however, took the idea more seriously than the Russians. The physical conditions of the prisoners were on the whole worse in the Siberian camps than in the Chinese ones; life in Siberia was inhuman and the physical suffering boundless, but the psychological pressure was less. There was time to think, to exchange ideas. In the midst of great physical deprivation the spirit was free – freer, even, than in the regimented society outside the camps. This was not the case in China. There the psychological pressure was kept up day and night. At public confession meetings the inmate had to expose his thoughts in the Criticism and Self-criticism learned from Stalin. This was practised throughout society, in offices and factories. In the closed atmosphere of the labour camps it proved lethal, killing all personal ideas, killing a person's inner conscience. There were some who resisted, who refused to accuse their cellmates, individuals who did not bend, but they often had to pay heavy penalties, solitary confinement or death. These meetings were also accusation meetings, the dreaded *kung-su hui* (gungsu hui). The person, or persons, to be accused were designated by the guards. There you were, standing with head bent, while all around, one after another of your companions shouted abuse at you. Nobody who cared for his own life dared to say a word in your favour. You were a public pariah, a target for blows, to be hit not by the guards but by your fellow-prisoners who thus had to manifest their virtue. You might be hung up by your hands, as happened to a Shanghai Christian girl who now lives in the United States. At the end of the session, you collapsed on the floor and your cellmates dragged you away half-dead. If you were lucky, it was over; but all too often the procedure was repeated a few days later if you had not confessed all your sins, or if, like that Christian Shanghai girl, you had refused to deny your faith or to accuse your companions.

For many, all this was more than human strength could bear. Hence there were many suicides in the camps. Fellow-inmates took such news with indifference. Human feelings and the desire for revolt had died long ago. There were also public executions – as there were outside the camps. The body was often left lying in a public place and the inmates had to file past it to remind them of what might be their fate if they did not behave. Some, carried away by anger, did not behave. We know of cases in which men killed those who had betrayed them to the authorities.

Life everywhere, even in the camps, had its darker and brighter sides. In the early 1960s when millions were dying of starvation, as Peking admitted twenty years later, those inside the camps still got their regular meagre meals and so were better fed than the villagers outside the camps. Some camps were stormed by outsiders, asking to be let in to where food was still available.

There was a curious relationship between the guards and the prisoners. The guards, members of the Security, lived in the camps with their families, whereas the wives or husbands of the prisoners lived far away in their own towns or villages. The families of the guards got privileged treatment; their food was better and their children went to school in the camp itself. The abyss between the life of the inmates and of the guards was felt intensely; yet incidents which would be punishable by death rarely occurred.

As the term of an inmate's imprisonment neared its end, the days before release were anxiously counted. All too often; when the day came the prisoner was not released. When he was released – this was the universal rule – the prisoner was not set free; he remained in the camp farm or factory as a 'free man'. He got paid a wage for his work, and was allowed to visit his relatives, even if they lived in far-away cities, once or sometimes twice a year. Often this first visit was a painful experience. The released person would find the family living in extreme misery. They were relatives of a counter-revolutionary, and were therefore outcasts from society. They could not get decent jobs. When they fell sick, no hospital would admit them. The young members of the family could not get into a school, and nobody except members of similar counter-revolutionary families would marry them.

6

OUTSIDE THE CAMPS: PUBLIC SECURITY

The administration of the labour camps was supposed to be placed under the Ministry of Justice, but the guards were still members of the Armed Police, a special body detached from the army; its First Political Commissar is the Minister of Security of the day.

Armed Security, in one form or another, is one of the oldest institutions of the Communist Party. It is a police corps checking the movements of citizens. But it is still more. It is a body of specially-trained political agents who operate both inside the Party and outside it. Real power in China lies not with the Communist Party as such, but with the Security within the Party. Its paramount function is guarding the guardians.

GUARDING THE LEADERS

After a long period of inner-party fighting, and with the settling down of the Party leadership in Yenan in the middle of the 1930s, the leaders learned from Moscow how to organise a system of control. The members of a United States military delegation visiting Yenan saw no policemen and were impressed by what they thought to be an orderly democratic society. Only later did they learn that there was a concentration camp not far away from where they were staying.

The brutal treatment of Mao's enemies – attributed to his henchman K'ang Sheng (Kang Sheng), who learned his trade in the Soviet Union – was not revealed until forty years later. The organisation of repression in Yenan has never been fully revealed.

In 1987 General Li Lien-hsiu (Li Lianxiu), then commander of the Armed Police Troops, gave a short interview to the Communist press. Born in Shantung province in 1924, he joined the Communist army at the age of sixteen and worked his way up from the lowest ranks to the command of an army. 'Now', he said with a smile, 'I have another job: to protect railways, bridges and canals, and to be present day and night on land, sea and air, arresting political agents and protecting the border areas of the country.' He revealed that the Armed Police Troops had a long history. They started in the 1930s as a troop protecting the leaders and arresting the enemies. Then in 1949, when the People's Republic was established, they were renamed Central Security Troops, and in the following years the name changed nine times. When General Li was asked how the troops protect the leaders, he smiled and said that he was sorry but that was a state secret. What he could say was that it was a very tight organisation which was ready to react instantly to any trouble.[1]

In his short interview General Li made it clear that since the 1930s the Armed Troops had been in charge of the protection of Party leaders and had been entrusted, further, with the task of suppressing the opposition. The opposition here did not mean the Nationalist Government, then engaged in a long-drawn-out war of attrition with the Communists; the opposition to be dealt with was the opposition within the Communist ranks. His reference to the 1930s probably indicated the years after 1935. In 1935, after the disorderly flight to the west under Nationalist pressure – the Long March – Mao's regime was established in the wild west, in the north of the province of Shensi.

That armed troops protect the leaders was one of the well-guarded secrets of the Communist regime. It became evident only during the Cultural Revolution when, in the turmoil which affected even the inner core of the Communist Party, Mao Tse-tung had to rely on his personal guard and did so quite openly. It was not a personal guard in the normal sense of the word; it was a large organisation, whose members he sent around the country to investigate how things were going and to report back to him. He spent much time with them in person, and took care of their behaviour and their education. Their head, Wang Tung-hsing (Wang Dongxing), who had been one of the guards around Mao back in Yenan times, became one of the

[1]*PD*, July 31, 1955; *Wen Hui Pao* 文滙報, Hong Kong, July 12, 1987.

leaders of the Party. In 1970 when Party reorganisation began after the onslaught of the Cultural Revolution, Wang Tung-hsing and his troops were held up as models for the reorganisation of the Party. In October 1976, a month after Mao's death, Wang took the lion's share in the lightning arrest of the ambitious Chiang Ch'ing and her companions. In 1977 he became one of the four Vice-Chairmen of the Communist Party. Then, with the rise of Teng Hsiao-p'ing, his power went into eclipse.

For a few years nothing was heard of the central guard of the Party leaders. Then at the end of 1982 it reappeared with full publicity, in the form of the Armed Police Troops. This grew into a million-strong military force with its own schools, hospitals – a powerful organisation for the suppression of all internal enemies of the regime. To check foreign spies, another organisation was set up in 1983, the Ministry of State Security – a literal translation of the KGB. The Armed Police Troops, it was revealed without ambiguity in August 1985, came under the Party CC's Politico-Legal Committee.[2] This Committee was under P'eng Chen and his men, arch-conservative adversaries of Teng Hsiao-p'ing. When P'eng Chen became head of the People's Congress in 1983, he handed over the job to Ch'en Pi-hsien. In 1985 Ch'en was succeeded by Ch'iao Shih, who in 1987 became one of the five-man Standing Committee of the Politburo, the highest ruling body of the Party. Ch'iao Shih, a man scarcely known even inside China, was born in 1925, entered the Party at the age of sixteen and is a long-standing member of the dreaded intelligence establishment.

A Disciplinary Committee was established inside the Party in December 1978 under Ch'en Yün, but it turned out to be too weak to re-establish Party discipline. In 1987 two *People's Daily* articles, one in January and the other in March, urged that in face of widespread abuses of power by Party members, inner-Party supervision should be strengthened and that the power of the Disciplinary Committee should be increased.[3] In November,

[2]*PD*, Aug. 17, 1985; and Ladany, *The Communist Party of China and Marxism, 1921–1985*, op. cit., pp. 394–6.

[3]*PD*, Jan. 25, 1987, p. 4; and March 3, 1987, p. 4.

after the 13th Party Congress, Ch'iao Shih took over the job from Ch'en Yün.

The history of inner-Party discipline also goes back to the Yenan days. The body in charge of it was euphemistically called the Social Affairs Department (*She-hui-pu*). Party history books, even those written forty years later, have kept silent about this intelligence organisation; its existence has been mentioned only once, in the 1950 'People's Handbook', published in Shanghai. Its head at that time was Li K'e-nung (Li Kenong).

In 1987 a Shanghai magazine, the *Wen Hui Monthly*, published the reminiscences of the daughter of Lo Jui-ch'ing, Minister of Public Security in 1949–59. She mentioned as a close friend of her father's this same Li K'e-nung (1898–1962), describing him as head of the Central Social Affairs Department in Yenan. She also said that before the establishment of the People's Republic, these two, Li and Lo, were the leaders of what was called the Security Department of the Central Committee's Military Committee, and that when the Communist regime was established, a Ministry of Security was set up in the Cabinet, headed by her father Lo Jui-ch'ing.[4]

GUARDING THE NATION

The Ministry of Security, set up in 1949, had overall control of the whole population. It had branches in every province, city and county. Under the Security were the sub-stations, i.e. the police stations, the much dreaded *p'ai-ch'u-suo* (paichusuo).

The Security and its police stations were given wide-ranging powers. A Regulation on Public Security was promulgated in October 1957. It described what appeared to be ordinary police work. The police were to keep order in government buildings and in public places. They were to stop pornography, prostitution, gambling, the making of fake official seals, the sale of fake

---

[4] *Wen Hui Monthly* 文滙月刊, Shanghai, no. 2, 1987, reprinted in *Hsin-hua Digest*, Peking, no. 5, 1987, pp. 156–61. Other sources have called Li K'e-nung head of the Central Liaison Office in Yenan, cf. *Handbook of United Front's Work* 統一戰線工作手冊, Nanking, 1986, p. 351.

drugs, fishing in forbidden waters and taking photographs in forbidden places. They were also to punish traffic transgressors and those who started fights, threw stones at trains, cars or shops, insulted people or used foul language, stole vegetables, fruit or agricultural implements, adulterated well water, threw rubbish on the streets and so on.[5]

In September 1986, the 1957 Public Security Regulation was replaced by a new Regulation. Like the 1957 document, it gave a detailed list of transgressions for which the police might impose fines the maximum of which was 20 yüan in 1957 and 200 yüan in 1980, or fifteen days' detention. Serious cases were to be referred to criminal procedure. The 1957 and 1986 Regulations were similar, but those of 1986 enumerated among the offences 'smoking opium, injecting morphine, planting poppies' (maximum fine 3,000 yüan), running brothels (maximum fine 5,000 yüan), damaging telephone lines and postal delivery, and concealing the discovery of historic objects.[6]

The 1986 Regulation, unlike that of 1957, mentioned corruption in the police force iself.

In the city of Shant'ou (Swatow) the head of the Security was purged for corruption, and in Shanghai the police were found to be importing pornographic videos into the country. In 1988 the provincial office of the Security in Chekiang province earned a considerable amount of money by issuing illegal exit permits in return for bribes. Thirty-five police stations in one of the counties of Hupei province were accepting bribes.

The prestige of the Security was not high. In Shenyang it discovered that functionaries in the city post office were making substantial sums of money by smuggling valuable cigarettes through the postal service. The post office responded by making accusations against the Security in the most public manner: namely, on the city's television channel. The whole affair went to Peking to the highest Party leadership. In many places, Wang Fang, Minister of Security, said, Security people and policemen carrying out their ordinary duty were being assaulted, beaten

[5] *Compilation of Selected Laws and Regulations on Security of the Chinese People's Republic*, op. cit., pp. 72–80.
[6] *PD*, Sept. 6, 1986, p. 2.

and wounded; a few were killed. Some of the victims claimed that they took action in self-defence.[7] Similar incidents occurred even after the T'ienanmen events of June 4, 1989. The Security offices in some cities in Ssuch'uan province were engaged in a big way in smuggling cigarettes from one province to another; tobacco is a state monopoly. In Shantung province the head of a city Security office was found to be corrupt and was arrested. Corruption cases were reported from Fukien, Kuangtung and Shansi provinces.[8]

It may be argued that such abuses were the exception, and that the bulk of the Security was working in orderly fashion. But was the Security and its police able to maintain its presence in this vast country and reimpose discipline? A 876-km.-long highway connects K'unming, captial of Yünnan province, with the border of Burma. The road is crowded; trucks, cars, bicycles and horse-carts transport men and goods; over long stretches the traffic moves at only 10 km. per hour because of the poor quality of the roads. On the roads, even after the events in T'ienanmen Square in June 1989, life was a free-for-all. Thousands of inns were serving food and drink and lodging – and many other things, smugglers, thieves and girls engaged in prostitution. The police were unable to act and keep control.[9]

The *villages* form an immense ocean in China. The country has 3.94 million of them grouped in 69,000 administrative units called *hsiang* and as of 1989 these in turn are grouped in 1,986 'counties' or *hsien*. The Security and its police had no presence in the villages: the lowest level of police stations were in the county towns. Public order in the countryside was supposed to be maintained by the Party organisations. In many villages even these were absent.

During the more relaxed decade between 1978 and 1988, when the use of land was given back to the farmers and money took the place of Party discipline, the village Party organisations and village governments in many places existed in name only,

[7] *Ming Pao* 明報, Aug. 20, 1986; *PD*, Aug. 14, p. 4; Aug. 28, p. 4; and Sept. 26, 1988, p. 3.
[8] *PD*, June 3; Aug. 5, 15 and 18, 1989.
[9] *PD*, Sept. 16, 1989.

a fact that was aired at a meeting of the Standing Committee of the People's Congress in 1989.[10]

According to Cabinet regulations, the police of the Security were responsible for order on all the roads of the country. This was to stop the abuse of the localities raising levies on vehicles passing through. However, the regulations could not be implemented. Villages, counties and even provinces issued their own regulations. Levies were still being raised, and the local police itself got its share of the extra income.[11]

Imperceptibly the villages, left to themselves, returned to the old system of electing their own elders and managing their own affairs, as they had done before the Communist regime. That this was so is confirmed in an article of the May 1989 issue of the fortnightly review of the Central Party School.[12] A 1986 report on a large county of 890,000 inhabitants, P'ingchiang county in the north-east of Hunan province, said that the ancient clans were ruling the villages, electing their local heads, rebuilding the ancestral halls, drawing up the traditional family-tree records and restoring the tombs of ancient historic figures of the county. Things were once more as they had been before the Communist regime. Public order was maintained by the people themselves, not by the Communist Party and its Security organs,[13] for whom there was hardly any need in such regions. But in other regions crime became endemic. Peasant gangs were halting and robbing freight trains, and fighting for cotton and silk-cocoons. In the vast ocean of rural villages, with their population of more than 800 million, isolated incidents of this kind did not threaten the political security of the state.

The *cities* were different. Popular uprisings there could threaten the survival of the regime, and so security there had to be maintained at all costs. The cities and towns had strong contingents of the Security. All were under the Ministry of Security – which itself was under the Politico-Legal Section of the Party's Central

[10] *PD*, Aug. 31, 1989.
[11] *PD*, Nov. 15, 1989.
[12] *Ch'iu Shih*, no. 10, May 16, 1989, p. 36.
[13] *Fa-hsüeh*, no. 4, 1986, pp. 16–18.

Committee. Each part of each city was ruled by its '*p'ai-ch'u-so*', – its police stations. However, the *p'ai-ch'u-so* is not a police station in the Western sense of the word. It controls, or is supposed to control, the lives of the people. It was expected to know everything about every citizen; who lived where, the size of each family, and the occupation and past history of each family member, which even included the family's friends and visitors. '*P'ai-ch'u-so*' officials visited the families regularly and asked polite questions. This questioning, however, could have unpleasant consequences.

The control of the urban population takes many forms. Ever since the start of the regime in 1949, the city streets have been organised into what were at first called Street People's Conferences. In 1951 these were renamed Residents' Committees and Street Bureaux, each of which controlled about 600 households. Under the Residents' Committees were the Small Groups, each in charge of from fifteen to forty households. Each one of the small groups sent a representative to the Street Bureau.

The police stations were responsible for suppressing counter-revolutionaries, preventing other crimes, supervising those condemned to surveillance, and registering households. They also controlled 'theatres, movies, hotels, radio sets, explosive materials and letter-carving'. Letter-carving means making seals, something which is ubiquitous in China, with personal names or names of organisations inscribed on them. These had to be strictly controlled. The police stations also had to direct the work of what were called Security Protection Committees, residents' organisations which had to report suspicious movements of people.[14]

In January 1958 a Regulation on the Registration of Households ordered every household to keep a 'household booklet' containing the particulars of each person. Change of domicile was allowed only if one obtained a permit. Staying temporarily in another place required a temporary permit. The form and content of the household booklet had to follow the uniform prescription of the Ministry of Security. In villages where there were no

[14] *CNA*, no. 70, Feb. 4, 1955.

police stations, the local authority of the village, the People's Committee, would be in charge of the registration of household members. Dormitories for government offices, schools, enterprises and other organisations were treated as households; in each a special person was in charge of personal registration.[15]

In 1985 an article on residence registration referred to this 1958 Regulation and said, what had not been said in 1958, that residents' permits were divided into six categories. These related to:

— the three cities – Peking, T'ienchin and Shanghai;
— other great cities;
— middle-sized and small cities;
— towns and boroughs;
— suburbs of cities and of boroughs;
— villages.

This rigid system, it was said in 1985, had the good effect of preventing a flow of migrants from the villages to the cities. On the other hand, it was admitted that its rigidity impeded the development of the economy and the development of towns and smaller cities.[16]

During the Cultural Revolution the army took over the Ministry of Security, the whole country being then in turmoil. In January 1974, Hua Kuo-feng became Minister of Security. The street organisations were reorganised under the militia into what were called Courtyard Management Committees. Their duty was 'to implement total dictatorship and to prevent the courtyards from becoming hotbeds of the bourgeoisie' and 'to criticise the anti-Marxist trend that was rearing its ugly head'. Children were organised into groups to study Marxism and sing revolutionary songs.[17] In 1980, under the regime of Teng Hsiao-p'ing, the old Regulation on mass organisation of public auxiliaries was re-published unchanged.[18]

[15] *Compilation of Selected Laws and Regulations on Security of the People's Republic of China*, pp. 83–7.
[16] *She-hui k'e-hsüeh* 社會科學 (Social Sciences), Shanghai, no. 6, 1985, p. 36.
[17] *CNA*, no. 1005, July 4, 1975.
[18] *Compilation of Selected Laws and Regulations on Security of the People's Republic of China*, pp. 218–20.

In the mean time, however, China had changed. More freedom in trade was allowed: the peasants brought their produce to the cities and sold it there, and business agents of government and private firms operated throughout the country. With such changes, discipline and surveillance had to be reintroduced.

In August 1987 a report spoke again of the establishment of mass public order organisations. According to this report, there were in 1987 1,170,000 public order committees divided into 3,050,000 small teams, with a total of 12 million people participating.

Of the 1.17 million public order committees, 728,000 were in the villages with 7.62 million members, 154,000 in the cities, and 290,000 in factories and mines.[19] With what we saw above about the villages where even the Party organisations were in disarray, one may suspect that those figures were plans only and existed only on paper.

Before 1979, before the introduction of Teng's liberal policy, the population was controlled by household registration. Nobody could move without a permit. When, however, millions moved from villages to towns and cities, control became loose. To check who was who, personal identity cards were introduced. Each card carries 15 figures, indicating province, area, county, date of birth and some unexplained data. By October 1, 1989 the carrying of identity cards had become compulsory, but hardly 10 per cent of the people obeyed this rule, and complaints of wrong entries of names were heard. By the end of November, 600 million cards were distributed, 83 per cent of the planned figure.[20]

The purpose of the system is clear. Every individual, certainly in the cities, is caught like a fly in a spider's web, entangled in its inter-crossing threads. Each person works in a 'unit', whether in a factory, a school or an office. He or she is also member of the Trade Union. Women are members of the women's organisation, and young people are members of youth organisations. One may be a Party member, as some 10 per cent of the adult

[19] ibid.
[20] PD, Nov. 11, 19, and 28, 1989.

population are, and thus under the discipline of the Party cell; but every single person is under the surveillance of the street organisations and above all, of the Security and its police stations.

Chinese are cautious by nature, and fear of what may happen tomorrow has a paralysing effect. The threads of the spider's web in which everyone is involved are fine, hardly visible. No outsider can see or hear what the Party secretary tells you. The head of the street committee, often a middle-aged woman with a taste for snooping into your family affairs, asks your neighbours about your unexpected visitor; the civilian-clothed man from the Security pays you a polite visit – that is enough to make you cautious, and put you on your guard, to make you pay heed to what you say and whom you meet. Your friends may not know why you suddenly turn shy and avoid them; a foreign professor teaching in the same school may wonder why you have stopped inviting him to your house. An American visitor whose father was a pastor in China may wonder why you carefully hide your Christian faith in the university compound where you live.

The fine threads tying you to the system, threads which may at any time turn into a rope, are not visible; but you know that that rope may drag you away from your family to unknown lands. You know perfectly well, as everybody knows, that anyone may be condemned to 'labour education', not by a court but, after denunciation by a colleague, by simple administrative measures.

From these indications one can see that under the wide-ranging economic reforms of the 1980s the system of control remained as it had been under Mao – indeed as it had been learnt from the Stalinist regime back in the 1940s, in Yenan days. The 1951 Regulation of Suppression of Counter-revolutionaries was still in force. Labour camps had not been disbanded, and people could still be sent to them by administrative measures. The Security organs still controlled households, and millions of civilians served as official informers. Armed police, cut off from the regular army, kept order and protected the leaders. The man in charge of all means of repression – through the courts, the Security, labour camps and the armed police – had become a member of the Politburo's Standing Committee, the highest ruling team of the country. This was the head of the Politico-Legal Branch of the Party, Ch'iao Shih.

The regime has many other means at its disposal for controlling social life. There is the Central Committee's United Front Department (hereafter UFD), a typically Chinese institution, a subtle means of controlling the nation. The Soviet Union had a Common Front policy, but this affected foreign relations only. The pro-Moscow international review, *Problems of Peace and Socialism*, which served eighty-two Communist parties throughout the world, contains many reports that dealt with the problem of common-front cooperation with non-Communist organisations in non-Communist countries. But inside the Soviet Union there was no 'common front' policy and the CPSU had no UFD.

In China, winning over people outside the Party, co-operating with them and deceiving them, has become a subtle art. Early in the 1940s Mao promised full democracy and capitalism, and said that China would not follow the Soviet system. After the Communist take-over, non-Communist sympathisers were honoured and asked to co-operate. In the late 1950s it became clear that this was a trap, but by then it was too late. The United Front policy continued.

The UFD of the Party deals with, and rules, the national minorities, which, small in number, inhabit the western and southwestern regions, two-thirds of Chinese territory. It also deals with religions, all of which are organised under this department. It is impossible to distinguish nationality and religion among the Muslims and the Lamaists – the influence of the Dalai Lama reaches to Inner Mongolia, a few hundred miles from Peking. Other religions too – Buddhism, Taoism and Christianity – are governed by the UFD; at the national conferences of each, a head of the department dictates policy.

Then there are the small political parties, the Democratic Parties, which, as has been repeated ever since the early days, come under the tutelage of the Communist Party. Small in membership and with no political muscle, they are the auxiliaries of the Communist Party, organising intellectuals, former businessmen and teachers. Their leaders are veteran Communist Party members whose Communist identities are revealed only at their funerals.

Some idea of the range of activities of the UFD may be gained from a book which it obligingly published itself in 1986. Its 866 pages contain a chronology of events from 1921 to 1986, 150 pages of short biographies of some 2,400 persons, 50 pages of terms and well-explained slogans, a list of organisations in which the UFD is interested, and a good description of Hong Kong and Taiwan, which were among the UFD's main targets in the 1980s. In other words, it is a mine of information on the wide domain of the UFD. Among the organisations under its authority are the Confederation of Chinese Women, of Youth and of Students, the Academy of Science, the Academy of Social Sciences, the Association of Scientists, the Federation of Literature and Art, Chinese PEN, the Association of Newspapermen, the Organisation of Sports and the International Travel Bureau. Also listed are the overseas editions of the *People's Daily* and the periodicals published in foreign languages in China.[21]

HEADING FOR TROUBLE

The whole system of control worked well for a long time, but something cracked within the system.

In the ten years from early 1979 to late 1988, the policies of economic reform had apparently resulted in an enormous success. The average real growth rate in the Gross National Product (GNP) for these ten years stood at 8.33 per cent annually. Between 1979 and 1985 alone, grain production increased from 304.75 to 378.98 million tonnes, i.e. by 24.4 per cent, which meant a 13.8 per cent increase of *per capita* grain production. It then rose even further to 402.41 million tonnes in 1987, so that the overall increase over ten years amounted to 32 per cent, raising production *per capita* by 17.2 per cent.[22] Growth-rates in industry, particularly for light and consumer goods, were even more impressive.

---

[21] *Handbook of United Front's Work*, op. cit.

[22] 1978: Hsüeh Mu-ch'iao (ed.), *Chung-kuo ching-chi nien-chien 1982* (Almanac of China's Economy, 1982), Economic Management Publishing Corporation, Peking, 1982, parts 8, 5 and 16 f; 1985: *PD*, Feb. 24, 1988.

China's share in world trade more than doubled from 0.8 per cent in 1978 to 1.7 per cent in 1988. Personal income was also showing a remarkable rise, and the gap between rural and urban income was closing from a ratio of 1: 3.14 in 1978 to 1: 1.89 in 1985.[23]

In 1985, however, the first signs appeared indicating that the country was moving into an economic crisis. This then developed fully during the first half of 1988, assuming the dimensions of a crisis involving the whole of society by the second half of 1988. The economy started to overheat, with a real GNP growth rate of 11.2 per cent in 1988. However, this growth was uneven. While the industrial production showed a real growth of 17.7 per cent, grain production fell from 402.41 million tonnes in 1987 to 394.01 million tonnes in 1988, i.e. by 2.1 per cent, which meant a *per capita* decline in grain production by 3.5 per cent.[24] Since the mid-1980s, income differentials were steadily widening. By the end of 1988, the relation between rural and urban income had widened again 1: 2.05.[25] Overall, the Gini coefficient for the People's Republic had risen from between 0.38 and 0.43 in 1978 to between 0.44 and 0.47 in 1987.[26]

Moreover, there was severe inflation. The officially announced inflation rates had been 8.8 per cent in 1985, 6 per cent in 1986, 7.9 per cent in 1987 and 18.5 per cent in 1988.[27] In fact, one has to assume an inflation rate of between 30 and 35 per cent for 1988, and the official figure was up to 27 per cent by May 1989.[28] The victims of these dramatic price increases were mainly industrial workers, teaching personnel on all levels of education, and a large portion of the intelligentsia. Even according to official data, 34.9 per cent of all urban households suffered a decrease in real

[23] 1978 and 1985: ibid.

[24] Computed from data published in *PD*, March 1, 1989.

[25] ibid.

[26] For 1978: William Parish, 'Egalitarianism in Chinese Society' in *Problems of Communism*, Washington DC, vol. 30, no. 1, Jan./Feb 1981, 41. For 1987: Computed on the basis of more than 1,400 data from different official PRC media sources.

[27] *PD*, March 1, 1986; Feb. 21, 1987; Feb. 24, 1988; and March 1, 1989.

[28] *PD*, May 9, 1986.

income in 1988.[29] Theoretically, this applied also to the cadres in the Party and the state administrative machines, but they had always been able to improve their income by taking bribes and accepting 'gifts'.

Since 1980/1 this tendency had become stronger, and since early 1987, the country experienced a veritable explosion of bribery, embezzlement and other illegal ways of increasing personal wealth. This occurred at all levels of Party organisation and state administration, and permeated the whole system to such a degree that, without doubt, China became in the late 1980s the most corrupt social body in the whole of East and Southeast Asia. When the Communist Party media revealed that during 1988 more than 45,700 cases of corruption had been investigated and tried by the courts, involving 8,777 cadres,[30] this was only showing the tip of an iceberg.

Such indications of increasing economic and social decay were aggravated by the fact, evident from the early and mid–1980s onwards, that the Marxist-Leninist doctrine had lost its motivating force for ever larger sections of the Chinese people.

The peasants had mostly experienced the core element of the policies of economic reform enacted by Teng Hsiao-p'ing and his associates since 1979 – the decollectivisation of agricultural production within the framework of a continuation of collective ownership of the arable land – as a great personal relief. Those of them who profited from the new rural policies mostly continued to support the ruling élite, even if only for the sake of their personal interest provided that these policies did not change – which many peasants feared, and seemingly continue to fear. However, such support was not expressed in any political activity, and even less in any belief in the doctrine of the Communist Party, but rather in making the utmost use of all chances of an improvement of individual living conditions.

Engineers, foremen and the more highly paid of the urban workers also profited up till 1987 from the policies of economic

[29] PD, March 1, 1989.
[30] PD (overseas edition), March 30, 1989.

reform. Yet the impact of inflation brought about a gradual erosion of their trust in the Party and its doctrine. This became even more true of the workers in the middle and lower wage-brackets. Having developed very high expectations during the initial stages of economic reform, many of them became increasingly disappointed. Hence, this group ceased to believe in the ideology of Marxism-Leninism and started to display a rising propensity towards dissent. The same is true of the urban poor – handymen, temporary workers and beggars – except that they were so caught up in their daily struggle to secure the most basic necessities of life that they had neither the time nor the energy for dissent.

The new private entrepreneurs in China were the group which, with the sole exception of the upper- and middle-income peasantry, profited most from the policies of the reform-oriented revisionists within China's Marxist-Leninist leadership. Yet because they were incessantly busy making money, they were afraid that a return to stricter concepts of socialism could endanger their very existence. Hence, while supporting the policies of economic reform, they were on the whole sceptical towards the doctrine of Marxism-Leninism. Moreover, they were put under increasing pressure from cadres demanding bribes, and often their lives were made difficult by those activists of the Marxist-Leninist party if they considered the bribes to be too low. Other small entrepreneurs suffered from the high rents which were levied if they operated state-owned 'means of productions' – such as taxi-cabs and trucks – on a contractual basis.

However, the most negative attitudes towards the Party were to be found among the young. The majority of the urban youth, and apparently an increasing number of young people in the more affluent village areas as well, cared only about having a career and enjoying life to the greatest extent that their still very limited means allowed. Already since the early 1980s, many young people adopted an attitude of total cynicism towards the doctrine of Marxism-Leninism, and thus a spiritual and moral crisis had spread among the young generation, particularly in the cities and among the students.[31] This situation was also reflected in the increasing reluctance among young people to join the Communist Party as members.

By the second half of the 1980s, the Marxist-Leninist ideology had thus run into a severe crisis. It had become stale and it had lost its credibility, so that, apart from about 800 persons forming the ruling élite, and an uncertain number of orthodox stalwarts among the Party cadres and members, hardly anybody in China any longer believed in Marxism-Leninism in 1988. Ideological apathy, cynicism and an ever-growing opposition to the Party doctrine had developed into a trend.

Faced with a major economic crisis, and with the erosion of the legitimising ideology, the ruling élite was confronted in the summer of 1988 with the problem of whether it should try to solve the crisis by introducing further and even more audacious economic reforms or by freezing these reforms at the stage which they had currently reached. During the debate of this question, the consensus on issues among the leadership dissipated.

At a 'Work Conference' of the Politburo and the Standing Committee of the Central Advisory Commission of the Communist Party, which convened in the second half of July 1988, in the Northern Chinese beach resort of Peitaihe, the reform-oriented revisionists under the leadership of the Party Central Committee's Secretary-General,[32] Chao Tzu-yang (Zhao Ziyang), confronted the orthodox group led by Prime Minister Li P'eng, First Vice-Premier Yao Yi-lin, and the Chairman of the Central Advisory Commission, the increasingly influential Ch'en Yün. Chao suggested countering the economic crisis with a radical unfreezing of almost all prices and a further limitation of the powers of the central planning organs. His proposal, however,

---

[31] Cf. Thomas P. Gold, 'China's Youth: Problems and Programs' in Chang Ching-yü (ed.), *The Emerging Teng System: Orientation, Policies, and Implications* (Institute of International Relations, T'aipei, 1983), part IV-2, 1–24.

[32] It should be pointed out that the Secretary-General of the Central Committee of the Chinese Communist Party is *not* in a position comparable, say, to that of the General Secretary of the Communist Party of the Soviet Union. He is not the 'Party Leader', but the person in charge of the administrative work of the civilian Party machine. The Chinese Communist Party is collectively led by the Standing Committee of the Politburo, of which, to date, the Secretary-General is one among altogether six members.

was rejected by the majority of the conference. At this point, Ch'en Yün moved to dismiss Chao from his position as Secretary-General. This motion was not put to the vote, but the conference adjourned until mid-August.

When it re-convened, Ch'en and Teng Hsiao-p'ing had worked out a compromise. The motion to dismiss Chao was withdrawn, but it was decided that the special responsibilities within the Politburo's Standing Committee should be re-assigned: Chao had to cede the responsibility for economic policies to Li P'eng and Yao Yi-lin.[33] Based on a draft prepared by Li and Yao, the third Plenum of the 13th CP/CC Congress, which convened in Peking from September 29 to October 1, decided to put the brakes on the policies of economic reform. Under the slogan 'Deepen the reforms, improve the economic environment, and restore economic order!', the plenum called for drastic cuts in investments, particularly in construction projects, and for a strengthening of the elements of centralised planning.[34] A few days later, the Peking government introduced either fixed prices or price-ceilings for altogether 326 groups of products, the prices of which had been unfrozen since early 1985.

Yet developments during the winter of 1988/9 proved that it was very difficult to implement these new decisions in the realm of economic policy. Many provinces were hesitant to execute them, some even flatly refused to do so, and on the local level, the degree of obedience to central directives decreased remarkably. Thus, a process of disintegration of the political system had begun to develop. It was further aggravated by an escalation of the inner-élite conflict over power and policies between the orthodox and the revisionist groups within the leadership, and by rising social unrest.

Such social unrest was strongly promoted by the impact of

---

[33] See the reports of 'Lo Ping' in *Cheng-ming* (Debate), Hong Kong, no. 130, Aug. 1988, 6–10; and no. 131, Sept. 1988, 6–11. Cf. James F. Sterba, 'Long March: How the Twisting Path of China's Reform led to Guns of Tiananmen' in the *Wall Street Journal*, New York, June 16, 1989.

[34] 'Communiqué of the third plenum of the Thirteenth CP/CC', Oct. 1, 1988 , in *PD*, Oct. 2, 1988.

inflation. Even wage rises, increased bonuses, and large handouts of inflation relief payments could not arrest the decline of the real incomes of all urban citizens who were continuously employed on the public payroll. These included workers and employees of all state-owned enterprises, comprising, in 1988, 88 per cent of urban labour:[35] scientists, university instructors and school-teachers, journalists, most medical personnel, many artists and writers, and the cadres of the Party and state administrative machines. But only the last category were able to balance their loss of real income by taking bribes and resorting to embezzle-ment. Thus, the ruling élite lost almost all the support which it still enjoyed among some urban groups until 1988.

Furthermore corruption in Party ranks, the economic reforms and a total lack of discipline led to a frightening increase in criminality. The official press reported groups of villagers stealing equipment from mines, railways and oil wells, and the robbing of freight from trains in not one but several provinces. It reported gangs of robbers attacking passengers in trains, armed gangs terrorising people waiting in line to buy movie tickets, highway gangsters, mass looting of ancient tombs, roving bandit gangs in the provinces along the Yang-tzu, the stealing of telephone lines, 2,000 peasants attacking a store selling fertiliser, 1,000 attacking a county government, girls being forced into prostitu-tion, the selling of women, and so on.

In February 1988 a deputy head of the Supreme Court spoke about the hazards which were being caused to communications with the cutting of wires along the railways, the destruction of signal lamps along waterways, and the removal of aviation signals; serious accidents had taken place as a result. People believed that public utilities could be taken away for their own personal use, he said.[36] He did not point out that such crimes were unknown before the Communist regime, or that the moral texture of the nation, the millennary consensus on basic moral principles, had crumbled.

---

[35] *PD*, March 1, 1989.
[36] *PD*, Feb. 6, 1988.

The reporting of such crimes, and of major accidents, was itself a novelty. Yet this openness had its limitations. Except in T'ienanmen Square in 1989, no television cameras, Chinese or foreign, ever reached the scenes of such events, and major disturbances and local revolts for example among the Turkic population in Sinkiang, were not reported. What was happening in Tibet was revealed by foreign visitors.

The highest authorities, however, were getting ready for major disturbances. In July 1988 at a National Conference of regional leaders of the Security, Premier Li P'eng said: 'There are some people who incite agitation, cause disturbances, carry out subversion and destruction' – words one often heard during the Cultural Revolution. 'To remedy this, it is necessary to hold fast to the People's Dictatorship and to hit hard at those who undermine political stability.'[37] In the same month Ch'iao Shih, when inspecting the three provinces of the north-east, said that the region was a hotbed of disturbances. Therefore 'the People's Dictatorship and politico-legal work should be strengthened, not weakened.'[38]

It is probably true, as the foreign press reported from Peking, that China sent agents to Poland, Austria and France to study anti-terrorist methods and that the first such specialised unit has gone into operation in China.[39] A year earlier, in June 1987, China joined the International Anti-Terrorist Convention, which obliged her to pursue terrorists taking refuge on its territory. The country also joined Interpol and a Chinese became its deputy head.[40] It was something new for a Communist country to have to learn from the West how to control its population, or rather to add Western methods to its own traditional arsenal of control. In January 1989 a brief news item said that in Peking a shock troop, founded in 1984, had been given an additional 780,000 yüan by the western district of the city.[41] It was not explained

[37] PD, July 6, 1988.
[38] PD, July 28, 1988.
[39] Agence France Presse in the *South China Morning Post*, Hong Kong, Aug. 9, 1988.
[40] PD, June 19, 1987, Dec. 1, 1987.
[41] PD, Jan. 8, 1989.

what these shock troops were, and whether they belonged to the military or to the armed police.

In March 1989 there was serious rioting in Tibet. High up in the Himalayas, this was far from the main body of China, but Peking took the rioting as a warning of what might happen throughout the rest of the country where, as was said, the growing inflation might cause social unrest. 'If unrest grows in a country, state and society may fall into turbulence and chaos . . . It has to be admitted that elements of disturbances do exist. This should not be taken lightly. If prompt action is not taken, what looks like a temporary disturbance may turn into great disturbance. What has happened in Lhasa shows this.'

This did not mean, as the speculation in Peking continued, that the reforms should be discontinued. We want socialist democracy, led by the Party Central, but it should be introduced gradually. Too much haste in introducing democracy might cause disturbances, and it would certainly not be proper to introduce the Western model. The Four Basic Principles must be maintained and social order safeguarded. Corruption within the Party and government should of course be fought on because these things caused deep resentment among the masses of the people. We must therefore introduce honesty in government and discipline in the Party and eliminate corrupt elements from both areas. This was said as editorial comment in the *People's Daily* in March 1989.[42]

Three days later the same publication referred to the flagging economy. 'There is tension over the provision of grain, cotton, edible oil, coal, power, petroleum and transport. If the bow is drawn too tight it may crack and the hearts of 1,100 million people may shudder. We are facing not merely an economic crisis but also a political crisis.' In addition, the country had millions of unemployed. In the previous few years 90 million peasants, redundant in the fields, had founded small factories in the villages and extended their trading into towns; this year 10 million more people were waiting for employment. Now with the economy

---

[42] *PD*, March 10, 1989.

cut back, millions were being returned to the villages, where they were idle. 'This is not merely a question of their livelihood; it is also a social problem.'[43]

Many of the unemployed, hundreds of thousands of them, left the inner provinces and travelled by train to distant places to the north-west, the north-east and Kuangtung province in the south. Trains were overcrowded, and people who failed to find jobs were roaming the streets, upsetting public order.[44]

T'IENANMEN

The above happened in the spring of 1989, six weeks before the students' demonstrations. The Party leadership was therefore well aware that there might be trouble. They expected it from the masses of unemployed workers, and they were afraid that the idea of democracy might spread. The Party of course has always spoken about democracy, but by that it has meant socialist democracy, democracy under Party rule or under the Four Basic Principles: Party rule, proletarian dictatorship, Maoism and Socialism. The view of the leaders was that Western ideas undermine 'socialist democracy', and they seemed to be ready to deal with major upheavals. They trained shock troops with anti-terrorist methods gleaned from Western Europe. They probably thought that they could face out any disturbances. Tibet was far away, an isolated area; when martial law was imposed there, it proved adequate to deal with the situation. Students in Peking, taking their lead from Peking University, the traditional hotbed of discontent, could cause trouble as they had done two years earlier at the beginning of 1987. The trouble had quieted down then, but it had had deep repercussions within the Party. What was called 'bourgeois liberalism' was strongly condemned, and the Party Secretary-General, Hu Yao-pang, was quietly dismissed and replaced by another of Teng's veteran assistants, Chao Tzu-yang. When things had quietened down, the reform movement

---

[43] PD, March 13, 1989.
[44] PD, March 6, 1989.

launched by Teng Hsiao-p'ing at the end of 1978 continued. Then Hu Yao-pang died on April 15, 1989 and the Peking students gave themselves over to demonstrations glorifying the memory of Hu as the champion of political reforms. This time the students did not calm down. They were further inflamed by the near advent of the seventieth anniversary of the never-to-be-forgotten May 4th Movement of 1919, a day that is looked upon as the birthday of a modern, westernised China. Next came the historic visit of Gorbachev. T'ienanmen Square was occupied by demonstrators, students from all over the country, and Gorbachev was unable to lay the customary wreath on the Heroes' Monument in the middle of the Square. All television-watchers could see that Teng Hsiao-p'ing was having difficulty in speaking; his speech war slurred. Next day, masses of demonstrators were shouting 'Hsiao-p'ing, you idiot.'

On the evening of May 19, in a dramatic turn of events, Li P'eng and Yang Shang-k'un (Yang Shangkun), President of the Republic and a leading member of the Military Committee, announced military intervention; the Party Secretary-General Chao Tzu-yang, was absent. The rupture in the Party leadership was evident. On May 20, martial law was declared and on June 3–4 came the massacre, watched on television by the whole world.

The sight of students being joined by the population of the city showed that something had happened that was without precedent in China's history. Not that revolt itself was new. But the April/May 1989 student demonstrations were quite different from the revolts of the past. It was a peaceful revolt. The city population joined in. Young children and old ladies came forward to assist the 2,000 fasting students. Many Party members joined the demonstrations and hundreds from the staff of the *People's Daily*, an organ of the CP/CC, marched under a great banner simply saying '*People's Daily*'. For some weeks people in Peking lived in a new world, with a vision of peace and freedom. It was a popular, unarmed, peaceful uprising in which the students took over the running of the city and the much-feared security police were nowhere to be seen. For four decades people in Peking had never known such peace and order, with mutual brotherhood proclaiming – as Ch'ai Ling (Chai Ling), a girl student leader put it – love and not hatred. All this provided an extraordinary vision of a China as it could be under a different regime.

It was on the whole not an anti-Communist, much less an anti-Socialist demonstration. People wanted a different style of government, and for a short while they enjoyed peace. For the first time in forty years, T'ienanmen, the square of Heavenly Peace, deserved its name. The demonstrations showed that a new generation had grown up in the civilised atmosphere of the universities where for ten years under the Teng regime the doors had been open to new ideas. Books on world culture were being published in great numbers. Thousands of scholars, Western and Chinese, had been invited to lecture. The Stalinist system and Marxism were open to criticism. Party heroes, Lei Feng and the rest, were ridiculed. The backwardness of China, compared with Japan, Taiwan and Hong Kong, became glaringly obvious. Chinese scholars took part in conferences in Hong Kong and in universities in the United States. A new generation was looking forward to a new China. These were the youngsters, many of them the children of Party leaders, who were dreaming of a civilised new world. They were incomprehensible to the older generation. Their fathers, now forty-five or fifty years old, had grown up during the Cultural Revolution, when Red Guards were fighting and killing one another, all in the name of Mao. Many of their highly-placed grandparents had fought the Nationalist regime with smoking guns. For these men, now getting old, the only known solutions to social problems were oppression and execution. They could not understand what the youngsters wanted. For them the student demonstration was a revolution against the regime and against the Communist Party; it was treason, it was counter-revolution.

FUTURE PERSPECTIVES

ANALYTICAL PREREQUISITES

by Jürgen Domes

The reasons for the spring crisis of 1989 were clearly recognisable, and they are now obvious: a strong wave of urban discontent with élite policy coincided with a major intra-élite conflict over power and policies.

The immediate results of the crisis itself were the violent suppression of the Democracy Movement, the victory of the orthodox faction and its strengthening by the change of position by Teng Hsiao-p'ing towards supporting its policies, and the PRC's move back in the direction of bureaucratic socialism of neo-Stalinist persuasion.

However, although the ruling élite, once again, succeeded in stifling a strong movement of the opposition, the massacres in Peking, Ch'engtu, Sian, Ch'angsha and probably also in other cities, and the campaign of terror which followed these massacres have destroyed the last vestiges of legitimacy which the Communist Party may still have commanded before June 4, 1989. Popular resistance has increased since the first week of June 1989. It merely assumes different features from those of the Democracy Movement in April and May of that year. One may, therefore, very well argue that the spring crisis of 1989 marked the beginning of the end of Communist rule in China.

Under these circumstances a review of the forces that can be expected to shape political developments in the PRC during the 1990s cannot be limited to the ruling élite, the Communist Party, and the People's Liberation Army. It has to take into account the opposition, and – last, but by no means least – the society as a whole.

The ruling élite and the Party. At an enlarged meeting of the Politburo which took place on June 19–21, 1989, the inter-élite conflict between the orthodox and the revisionist factions was eventually settled. This was ratified by the fourth Plenum of the 13th CP/CC, convening in Peking on June 23 and 24.[1] The purge remained confined to four leaders. Chao Tzu-yang and Hu Ch'i-li were dismissed from the Standing Committee of the Politburo, the Politburo itself and the Secretariat, and Jui Hsing-wen (Rui Xingwen) and Yen Ming-fu (Yan Mingfu) from the Secretariat. Thereafter, the inner leadership core, the Standing Committee of the Politburo, consisted of five orthodox politicians: the new Secretary-General of the CP/CC, Chiang Tse-min (Jiang Zemin) (65), Prime Minister Li P'eng (63), the leader of the security apparatus Ch'iao Shih (67), First Vice-Premier Yao Yi-lin (74), and the second newly appointed member of this body, Sung P'ing (Song Ping) (74). Only the sixth member of this group, the former Mayor of T'ienchin, Li Jui-huan (57), can be counted as a reformist-oriented revisionist. The Politburo as a whole now has only fourteen members and one alternate, nine of whom can be considered as orthodox[2] and only four as revisionist,[3] while the political positions of one member and of the alternate[4] remain unclear.

This, however, still does not provide a sufficiently precise picture of the factional line-up within the ruling élite. Since the spring crisis of 1989, the political influence of a number of veteran revolutionaries has greatly increased. Here, besides Teng Hsiao-p'ing (87) and Ch'en Yün (86), the two most influential leaders in the PRC, Vice-President General Wang Chen (Wang Zhen) (83), Sung Jen-ch'iung (Song Renqiong) (84), and the traditional Stalinists Li Hsien-nien (86) and Po I-po (Bo Ibo) (82) must be mentioned. With the exception of Teng, who supported the policies of economic, though not of political, reform, all of them have continuously tended to take orthodox positions, and it must therefore be expected that they will influence PRC politics in

---

[1] *PD*, June 25, 1989.

[2] Chiang Tse-min, Li P'eng, Ch'iao Shih, Yao Yi-lin, Sung P'ing, General Yang Shang-k'un (84), Li Hsi-ming (65), Li T'ieh-ying (Li Tieying) (55), and Wu Hsüeh-ch'ien (Wu Xuetian) (70).

[3] Li Jui-huan (73), Wan Li (73), T'ien Chi-yün (Tian Jiyun) (62), and General Ch'in Chi-wei (Qin Jiwei) (77).

[4] Yang Ju-tai (Yang Rudai) (65) and Ting Kuang-ken (Ding Kuanggen) (62).

the direction of a strengthening of central planning and strict discipline under the doctrine of Marxism-Leninism.

Time will take its toll among this group of rulers. It has to be expected that by the mid-1990s all or at least most of the veterans will have left the political scene due to their weight of years. If there should be no further major inner-élite conflict which brings about thoroughgoing changes of leadership personnel – a proposition which is by no means certain – this would leave the current Politburo members still at the helm of the Party by about 1992 to 1995. At the time of writing they have – if one includes the alternates – an average age of 67.73 years. But no clear distinction according to age can be made among the adherents of the two political tendencies, orthodox and revisionist. The nine orthodox Politburo members have now an average age of 66.44 years, the four revisionists of 65.75 years, and among the five youngest members, including the alternates, there are two orthodox, two revisionists and one whose position is unclear. This means that no drastic change of élite policies can be expected merely because of age. Moreover, a review of the fifteen youngest members of the CP/CC whose current position makes it likely that they may advance to the Politburo in the near future provides no additional clues. Six or seven of them must be considered orthodox and five or six revisionist, and the positions of three remain unclear.

One observation can be made with more confidence than the attempt to gauge future policy trends among the core élite. The events of May and June 1989 left the Party in a very difficult situation with regard to internal Party coherence and discipline. When, on May 24, the provincial Party leadership groups hastened to declare their support of the state of emergency, and hence their loyalty to the current leadership, six out of thirty provinces were conspicuously missing from the fold, among them the economically strong provinces of Kuangtung and Liaoning.[5] Here, future rifts may have been signalled already.

To sum up, within the Communist Party, inner-élite conflicts

---

[5] Chekiang, Kiangsi, Kuangsi, Kuangtung, Kueichou, and Liaoning. See *PD*, May 24, 1989.

are very likely to continue through the next 1990s. But dedication to the cause of Marxism-Leninism is not very widespread among its members, and the events in the spring of 1989 further weakened the morale of the Party, leaving it still an important force in the politics of the PRC, but nonetheless significantly weakened.

The military. It was the PLA which suppressed the Democracy Movement in Peking and other cities in the massacre of June 4, 1989. As already in the Cultural Revolution, particularly in January/February and from July till October 1967 as well as in the summer of 1968, and in the conflict over the succession to Mao Tse-tung with the military *coup d'état* of October 6, 1976, the PLA once again asserted its position as a decisive factor in crises of the PRC, and it can hardly be doubted that this will be the case in future crises too. However, one may well question whether the military will continue indefinitely to support the ruling élite in such periods of crisis.

There were some indications in later May and early June 1989, that there was opposition to the crackdown on the Democracy Movement within the Army. On May 22, seven retired generals enjoying high prestige with the PLA warned in a letter to the Party centre against employing the PLA to enforce the state of emergency declared on May 20.[6] Although this move was countered by an open letter of the Chief of General Staff, the Directors of the PLA General Political and General Rear Services Department, and six out of seven Military Area Commanders, declaring their full support for the emergency order,[7] difficulties did arise within the military in connection with the massacre. Such difficulties, however, did not yet pose a grave danger to the ruling élite. Yet there was scattered insubordination. In the province of Kirin, some units mutinied together with a number of their officers,[8] and in Peking there were soldiers and officers who took off their uniforms, changed to civilian clothes, and disappeared

[6] Text of this letter in *Chung-kuo shih-pao/China Times*, T'aipei (hereafter *CKSP*), May 23, 1989.
[7] *PD*, May 24, 1989.
[8] Radio Kirin, June 11 and 13, 1989.

during the night and the early morning hours of June 4.[9]

With the generational change in the military command positions which took place between 1985 and 1987, more professionally-oriented military leaders replaced the veterans of the 'Long March' and the civil war, who had a definite record of political involvement. The active top leadership of the PLA has currently an average age of about sixty-one years, with the oldest member of that group being aged seventy, the youngest forty-eight, and the overwhelming majority between fifty-eight and sixty-eight years of age. This means that, apart from the oldest and the youngest in this group, most of them were between nineteen and twenty-nine when the PRC entered the Korean War. Obviously, it is the generation of those who commanded platoons and companies in the Korean War which is now in active command. This generation is much more thoroughly educated in military techniques than its predecessors, and they have not hitherto displayed much active political interest. Thus, it is impossible to hazard estimates as to their future political attitudes. But it can be proposed with reasonable safety that the PLA will continue to be interested in the improvement of the military budget, which suffered drastic cuts in the 1980s, and that it may make such an improvement a condition for its continued support of the ruling élite. This, in turn, will put additional strain on an already rather constrained state budget.

However, support by generals and the officer corps does not necessarily also mean support by the rank-and-file, in particular, the conscripts who make up about half of all soldiers. For the rank-and-file professional soldiers and the conscripts, the steep decrease in the prestige of the PLA was a source of material and psychological difficulties already before the Spring Crisis of 1989. The peasant families of conscripts as well as those of professional soldiers were missing one working person, and thus received in many areas of the PRC less arable land to till. The low salaries of the soldiers made them less attractive matches than during

---

[9] Information provided to the author by citizens of the PRC in the United States, June and July 1989.

the 1960s and 1970s, when members of the PLA had enjoyed important privileges, particularly in the distribution of consumer durables, which later became rather commonplace. While peasant girls, for example, had been eager to marry soldiers in earlier times, they started shunning them after 1980/1. After the Peking massacre of June 4, the prestige of the PLA reached a very low point. Students began to call it the 'People's Liquidation Army' in English or – in a change of one character in the name of the military – 'Chung-kuo sha-min chieh-fang-chün' in Chinese, which can be translated as 'Chinese People's Killer Liberation Army'. The PLA is therefore a military force under severe psychological stress, and it is by no means a foregone conclusion that it will remain a loyal and ready tool for the use of the ruling élite once the next major political crisis erupts.

Party and army are, thus, both in a sensitive and not entirely reliable condition. Whatever their attitudes may be in response to being called upon for action by the élite, during the next decade, they are definitely no longer the only viable forces shaping politics in the PRC. Since the events of May and June 1989, the opposition circles have become part of any political equation.

The opposition. Although the PRC has a long history of dissent, climaxes of which were the 'Hundred Flower Campaign' in the spring of 1957, the wave of citicism directed at Mao Tse-tung by the Party intellectuals in 1960/1, the activities of radical 'Red Guard' groups in Hunan, Chekiang and Kuangtung in 1967/8, the anti-Maoist demonstrations in April 1976, and the Democracy and Human Rights Movement in 1978/9, opposition to the Marxist-Leninist single-party dictatorship was at best, very poorly organised for more than three decades.

It was during the early 1970s that the first nuclei for an opposi-tional network began to form. Gradually, a number of small urban circles evolved which combined the remnants of the 'Red Guard' organisations of the late 1960s with those forces of the Democracy and Human Rights Movement of 1978/9 that went underground when this movement was repressed in 1979/80. These circles actively opposed the policies of the ruling élite with a general platform calling for freedom of speech, information, assembly, and association as well as for competitive elections, i.e. for the introduction of elements of a participatory political culture into the subject culture of the official political society in the PRC.

Soon, these circles were joined by a number of students who had returned from advanced studies in Western countries, and after the repression of the Students' Democracy Movement of November and December 1986 by a considerable number of students from universities, colleges and senior high schools within the PRC. Since early 1987, workers too – in particular young ones – began to link up with these circles. Yet they had no national organisation, they were unco-ordinated, and until the spring of 1989 it appeared as if these circles still had a long time to wait until they could become a viable political force. It seemed safe to assume that the Communist Party, being the only nationally organised political force, would continue its rule unchallenged, if only by default of its active opponents.

During April and May 1989, however, the rudimentary local-ised beginnings of an organised opposition were overtaken by the vehemence of the Democracy Movement, within the context of which the opposition started to organise itself on a larger scale. First in Peking and soon in a number of other cities, 'Autonomous Federations' and 'Autonomous Unions' of students, workers, intellectual circles and even of government officials and journalists working in the official media were established, consciously fol-lowing the model of the Polish 'Solidarity' movement. These organisations established informal inter-regional contacts, and it appeared as if they were on the verge of forming a nationwide network, when the ruling élite started the suppression of the movement. The days between the proclamation of martial law on May 20 and the massacre in Peking on June 4, however, appear to have been used by the opposition groups to prepare for under-ground activities. Despite the official ban on the autonomous organisations, there are indications that these groups continue at least some of their activities, and that they are strengthening their contacts. At the same time, a large number of anti-Communist

Party organisations have been formed among the students and exchange scholars from the PRC working abroad, which seem to rally a majority of them, either openly defying the regime or clandestinely working against its policies.

Thus, the opposition has become somewhat more organised than it used to be before 1989. Yet even more important forces which are going to shape future political developments in the PRC are increasingly developing within society. In fact, it is these forces which turned the Democracy Movement in the spring of 1989 into more than just another abortive attempt to democratise China.

Society. In the 1950s, some of the more simplistic hypotheses which emerged from the theory of totalitarianism suggested that, in the so-called 'totalitarian states' an extremely efficient élite imposed its will upon a totally silent populace. However, observation of more than seven decades of Marxist-Leninist regimes, and of almost four decades of the PRC leads us to take a more differentiated approach to the explanation of inter-actions between élite and society in totalistic single-Party systems in general, and in the PRC in particular.

I have suggested that the seizure of power by élites oriented towards totalitarianism, and the stability of political systems established and dominated by such élites, depend upon the forging and sustaining of social coalitions or the ability of the élite to prevent the evolution of such coalitions directed against it. In any given society, all strata of the population develop specific hopes, expectations and desires. Elites are only able to seize power if they manage to respond to them, and in order to stay in power they have, at least occasionally, to renew such respon-siveness. The term 'social coalition' is defined here as a loose alliance that accumulates the demands of different strata of the society, demands which are usually, though not always, inherent rather than precisely enunciated.[10]

---

[10] For details, see Jürgen Domes, *The Government and Politics of the PRC: A Time of Transition*, Westview Press, Boulder, CO, and London, 1985, pp. 57–60 and 229–31.

Before the inflation and the ensuing disintegration of the society in 1987/8, the policies of the ruling élite were generally supported by a social coalition of leading cadres, a sizeable group of the mid-level cadres, the majority of the technological and scientific intelligentsia, engineers, the higher-paid industrial workers, and the newly-emerging private owners of small urban individual enterprises. Those peasants who profited from the decollectivisation of agricultural production, a proportion we may reasonably estimate at about two-thirds of the peasantry or approximately 47–48 percent of the Chinese population in the PRC, tolerated the current ruling élite as long as it guaranteed the continuation of its rural policies. Yet during 1988 and until the spring of 1989, one group after the other left the social coalition which till then had supported the ruling élite.

A rather formidable new social coalition evolved, which displayed an increasing propensity towards active opposition. It is now composed of almost the whole of the younger intelligentsia in the humanities, the majority of the technological and scientific intelligentsia, the students, many apprentices and young workers, most of industrial labour, the majority of employees in commerce and services, artists, writers, many journalists, and most of the owners of small individual enterprises. In other words: in the period since the spring of 1989, almost the entire urban society of the PRC has emancipated itself from the Party. The basic political contradiction today is no longer the contradiction between the ruling élite and small circles of poorly organised yet active oppositionists, but the contradiction between the ruling élite and the urban citizenry.

Indeed, the process of separation between the Party and society reached a quite advanced stage during and after the spring crisis of 1989. Yet there remains the question to what extent the 73 per cent of the PRC's population who live in the countryside, and particularly the 60 to 65 per cent who make their living by farming, have been affected by these fundamental social developments. Are they on the verge of a nationwide peasant rebellion? The answer is no. Despite more than three decades of political campaigns, mobilisation attempts, passive and even active resistance between 1950 and 1980/81, the Chinese countryside is still divided into approximately 6–7 million almost uncoordinated societies with nearly pure parochial political cultures. These minuscule polities have time and again successfully resisted all attempts to rally them in support of the ruling élite, but they have so far not been able to generate the momentum for a nationwide drive toward systemic change. There is not even a nucleus for an organisation that could aggregate and articulate peasant interest at a higher level than that of the village.

However, this does not mean that the countryside may not be affected by social unrest in the near future. Quite the contrary, this could happen locally and the government may be forced, by lack of funds, to pay for contracted grain at low prices with debit notes instead of cash. In this context, the quest of the peasants for title deeds to the land they now till individually under contract will most likely become very strong. And almost certainly it will soon be followed by the quest for freedom of childbirth. It can no longer be excluded that the peasants may confront the Marxist-Leninist rulers with these two demands in the not-too-distant future, and that could mean that the crisis of the political system of the PRC, which has become evident in the cities already, would also become evident in the countryside.

The conclusion from these findings seems to be that China's future can no longer be projected solely in terms of the continuation of Chinese Communist single-party rule.

PROJECTIONS

by Marie-Luise Näth

In the immediate future, which means in the next three to five years after the spring crisis of 1989, we cannot expect a return to 'normalcy', however this would be defined in the PRC. Under the impact of increased repression, the people will try to circumvent the political system and the demands of the ruling élite to an even higher degree than they already have during the last five years. They will use the propensity of the cadres to corruption to make the grip of the regime less oppressive by bribing its representatives. To give one example: Within less than four weeks after the Peking massacre, the newly-introduced special exit permits, which citizens of the PRC now have to obtain before they can apply for foreign visas, could be bought from corrupt cadres for 7,500 Yüan each in Shanghai, while in Canton, where the national currency is obviously no longer held in esteem, the price was US $2,000 or Hong Kong $15,000.[11]

Moreover, the people will increasingly try to move out of the system of the socialist economy into an ever-expanding parallel or second economy of moonlighting, black-marketeering, illegal exchange of foreign currency, underground banking and underground production. These trends are bound to weaken the structures of social control still further, even though the structures of political control may be strengthened for an intermediate period. This means that societal policies in general will be more and more difficult to implement. In particular, the birth-control and family-planning policies, which were already showing major deficiencies from 1986 onwards, and were verging on failure by 1988, will probably collapse, and the education and public health system will continue to deteriorate.

Even without taking into account the perspectives for the political system, the social and economic trends which can be expected for the 1990s leave little room for the ruling élite to feel optimism.

In July 1990, the official figure given for the population passed the mark of 1.13 billion. This figure, however, does not include between 25 and 35 million so-called 'black babies', i.e. children born in defiance of the ruling élite's family-planning rules and hidden from the authorities.[12] Even if the population growth-rate were to stay at the official figure of 1.43 per cent in 1988 till the mid-1990s, and then drop to 1.3 and further to 1.2 per cent, the PRC would have between 1.29 and 1.3 billion inhabitants

---

[11] Same sources as in note 9.
[12] This figure was first published by a journalist from the Republic of China on Taiwan after intensive research in the PRC in *CKSP*, Sep. 21, 1989. Later, PRC officials revealed the number of 1.8 million 'illegal' births in the year 1988.

by the year 2000, which means about 100 million more than
originally planned. But this figure may even grow to anything
between 1.35 and 1.4 billion. Population growth puts severe
limits on the prospects for economic development. The current
ruling élite, during the early 1980s, had set the goal of achiev-
ing a *per capita* GNP of US $800 at 1985 value by the end at the
1990s. This goal apeared realistic, but in order to reach it, real
per capita growth of the GNP must remain constant at 7 per cent
right through till 2000. Only if it were to stay at 8 per cent – a
rather unlikely long-term projection for the 1990s – could the goal
be surpassed, and the *per capita* GNP reach US $895. At 6 per
cent real growth annually, it would already reach only $757 by
the year 2000, and at 5 per cent, only $670. This perspective has
become quite likely, as the GNP growth rate had only reached 3.9
per cent in 1989.[13] But even if an annual *per capita* growth rate
of 7 per cent could indeed be sustained, this would bring the
PRC only to the level which South Yemen and Nicaragua had
reached in 1985. This means that the PRC will definitely remain
an underdeveloped country with very limited chances of accele-
rated modernisation until the end of this century and well beyond
that date. Moreover, it is not very likely that, within just a few
years, the ruling élite, ridden with political and social problems
as it is, will be able to solve the three major economic problems
which beset the PRC: inflation, shortage of energy and shortage
of raw and semi-processed materials, not to mention the annual
threat that a poor harvest could again set off at least a regional
famine.

In terms of social development, the prospects also appear
comparatively bleak. Even if there were the possibility that greater
economic changes could come about than one can expect now,
by the year 2000 at least two-thirds of the population will still
live in hamlets, villages and small towns in the countryside, and
between 50 and 55 per cent will still derive most of their income
from farming. In both the cities and the villages, income differentials will most probably widen further, as will the gap between

[13] *PD*, Feb. 21, 1990.

urban and rural income and that between the more well-to-do regions and the poor ones.

The history of the PRC hitherto has strongly suggested that the economic and social perspectives of the country depend on its political development much more than – as assumed by Marxism-Leninism – its political development depends upon developments in the economy and society. It is therefore of central importance to address the political trends which can be expected during the next decade, and that means to develop perspectives for the political system of the PRC in the form of alternative projections.

Theoretically, one such projection could be that if the ruling élite were to achieve a thoroughgoing success in stifling dissent once and for all, a stabilised system of bureaucratic socialism would evolve. In this case the ruling élite would definitely try to continue the policies of a selective and controlled opening towards the outside world, but in the domestic arena it would freeze the economic reforms at the level of 1988. However, since the Spring Crisis of 1989, the continuation of Marxist-Leninist single-party rule as a stable, institutionalised system well into the twenty-first century is most unlikely. As we have seen earlier, indications point to new crises within the PRC's ruling élite and between the Party and the society.

While Communist rule seems doomed to collapse in China, as well as elsewhere, the crucial question is how this might happen and for how much longer the agony of Communism will continue. Four alternative projections appear reasonably realistic and may provide a tentative answer to this question:

(1) It appears possible that we are facing a comparatively long period of repression under a predominantly orthodox leadership which would be mellowed by corruption on the one hand and by the continuous expansion of the parallel economy on the other. The society and the rulers would coexist in a state of mutual hostility. For the economic reforms, the parameters for individual enterprise, state enterprise autonomy, and decollectivised agricultural production would be frozen on the level of 1988, and

demands to widen them would be refused by the ruling élite. In order to sustain this refusal, the bureaucratic elements of the economy would tend to be progressively strengthened. However, the ruling élite would hardly be able to secure for its developmental designs either individual support or social loyalty. Therefore, social tensions would necessarily increase further and eventually explode in consecutive manifestations of ever more violent dissent. A number of such manifestations could probably be suppressed. But China would inevitably stumble into chaos and move toward a large-scale, extremely violent confrontation, which then would lead to the drowning of Communist rule in an ocean of blood.

(2) It is also possible that the reform-oriented revisionists could return and assume control of the decision-making organs of the Party state. In this eventuality, the new leaders would probably push ahead with further economic reforms, unfreeze all prices, decollectivise rural land ownership, remove most of the existing limitations on individual enterprise, and widen the parameters of state enterprise autonomy. Thoroughgoing economic reforms could be accompanied by political measures toward democratisation such as the raising of the level at which direct elections occur from the county to the provincial or even the national level, the introduction of free choice between several candidates in elections, and the granting of considerable autonomy to social organisations. But the expansion of economic reforms would certainly result in an acceleration of inflation and a further increase in income differentials. The Communist Party would have to bear the brunt of growing public discontent, and this would probably lead to a gradual edging of the Party out of power – a development very similar to that in Poland – and hence to a more or less peaceful transition from Communism to market-oriented pluralism.

(3) It could very well happen that if the reform-oriented revisionists were to return to power and attempt to expand the scope of the policy of reform, there would be a back-lash from

the orthodox forces, most likely in the form of a *coup d'état* backed by parts of the Army. This scenario would almost certainly result in another attempt by social forces to launch a nationwide movement against the ruling élite. It is possible that this time parts of the PLA would take sides with them, and eventually Marxist-Leninist single-party rule would probably collapse in a rather violent overthrow of the Communist Party.

(4) Finally, we might witness a speedy aggravation of the current economic crisis, which would combine with a leadership crisis after the disappearance of Teng Hsiao-p'ing, Ch'en Yün and other veteran revolutionaries. In these circumstances, or even if there were merely a new leadership crisis without the aggravation of the already precarious economic situation, opposition forces in the society could rise again. After the experience of the massacre of 1989, these forces would surely not only be prepared to offer effective resistance in their own defence but they would also be able to organise manifestations on a much larger scale than in the spring of 1989. In such a situation in which considerable parts of the PLA would also possibly no longer be willing to protect the rulers and fight the people, it could very well happen that within a couple of days or only a few weeks Communist rule in China would simply collapse, following the entire disintegration of the control structures and the sudden disappearance of the leadership personnel. There would be some bloodshed, but on the whole the process of transition from Communism to market-oriented pluralism would be peaceful.

Of course, it is not merely difficult to venture the allocation of probability ratings to these four projections, such an attempt is also completely beyond the capacity of a social scientist. However, it is obvious that the fourth projection remains realistic only for a very limited period of time, for at most three to five years after the Spring Crisis of 1989. On the other hand, the first projection gains in probability the more time passes by without the development of major new difficulties in the economy and conflicts within the current Communist Party leadership. But the question how and when Communist rule in China comes to an end, in particular the question whether this might occur very soon, depends ultimately on how China's people view their present situation in the perspective of their experiences of Communism during more than four decades. An inexperienced foreign observer would tend to think that the overwhelming majority of the Chinese people in the PRC were never better off than in the period after the introduction of reform policies and opening towards the outside world – and would therefore not expect an abrupt uprising of the masses. However, it may well be that in the perception of the overwhelming majority of the PRC's citizens the years of Communist rule have been one protracted ordeal. This is, indeed, what Father Ladany seems to suggest in this book. For China, as he says, has witnessed many periods of turbulence in its history and as a rule these periods have lasted for several decades, sometimes even for centuries, without permitting law and legality to guide political and social life. But it needed a Communist ruling élite in China to make lawlessness a guiding principle of political and social normalcy. Never, before the establishment of a People's Republic, was there an undisputed and hence politically strong central leadership in China which, instead of bestowing rules upon the Chinese, deprived the individual of even the smallest scrap of security and right. While in the pre-European Chinese Middle Ages the restoration of political and social normalcy through the establishment of central leadership used to be followed immediately by new law codes, European modernity in the names of Marx, Engels, Lenin, Stalin and Mao Tse-tung confronted China's population with despotism of unprecedented proportions. It therefore appears doubtful whether, for an ordinary Chinese citizen, anything about the People's Republic seems worth defending after more than four decades of Communist rule. In reality an uprising of the Chinese masses could happen at any time.

SELECT BIBLIOGRAPHY

Note. This bibliography contains only books published before 1960 which can be considered classics, and the major standard literature on developments after 1949 which has since been published in English or French. Its aim is to give the non-specialist reader a first introduction to the most relevant literature.

Bergère, Marie-Claire, Lucien Bianco and Jürgen Domes (eds), *La Chine au XXe siècle*, 2 vols, Fayard, Paris, 1989–90.

Bielenstein, Hans, *The Bureaucracy of Han Times*, Cambridge University Press, 1980.

Bodde, Derk, *China's First Unifier: A Study of the Ch'in Dynasty as seen in the Life of Li Ssu*, E.J. Brill, Leiden, 1938.

Cheng, Chu-yüan, *China's Economic Development: Growth and Structural Change*, Westview Press, Boulder, CO, 1982

Chiu, Hungda, *Chinese Law and Justice: Trends over Three Decades*, no. 7, Occassional Papers/Reprint Series in Contemporary Asian Studies, University of Maryland Law School, Baltimore, 1982.

Chow, Tse-tsung, *The May Fourth Movement*, Harvard University Press, Cambridge, Mass., 1960.

Copper, John F., Franz Michael, and Yuan-li Wu, *Human Rights in Post-Mao China*, Westview Special Studies on East Asia, Boulder, CO, 1985.

De Bary, William Theodore, Wing-tsit Chan, Burton Watson, (comps.), *Sources of Chinese Tradition*, Columbia University Press, New York, 1960.

Dittmer, Lowell, *China's Continuous Revolution: The Post-Liberation Epoch, 1949–1981*, University of California Press, Berkeley, 1987.

Domes, Jürgen, *The Internal Politics of China, 1949–1972*, C. Hurst, London, 1973

——, *The Government and Politics of the PRC: A Time of Transition*, Westview Press, Boulder, CO, 1985.

——, *China after the Cultural Revolution*, C. Hurst, London, 1977.

—— (ed.), *Chinese Politics after Mao*, University College Cardiff Press, Cardiff, 1979.

Eichhorn, Werner, *Chinese Civilization: An Introduction*, Praeger, New York, 1969.

Fung Yu-lan, *A History of Chinese Philosophy*, trans. Derk Bodde, Princeton University Press, 1952.

Gernet, Jacques, *A History of Chinese Civilization*, trans. J.R. Forster, Cambridge University Press, 1982

Harding, Harry, *China's Second Revolution: Reform After Mao*, Brookings Institution, Washington, DC., 1987.

Hinton, Harold C., *An Introduction to Chinese Politics*, Praeger, New York, 1973.

———, *Communist China in World Politics*, Houghton Mifflin Co., Boston, 1966.

Hsiao Kung-ch'uan, *Rural China*, University of Washington Press, Seattle, 1960.

———, *A Modern China and A New World: K'ang Yu-wei, Reformer and Utopian*, University of Washington Press, Seattle, 1960.

Hsieh Pao-chao, *Chinese Government, 1644–1911*, Johns Hopkins University Press, Baltimore, 1935.

Ladany, Laszlo, *The Communist Party of China and Marxism, 1921–85: A Self-Portrait*, C. Hurst, London, 1988.

Leng, Shao-chuan, *Justice in Communist China: A Survey of the Judicial System of the Chinese People's Republic*, Oceana Publication, Dobbs Ferry, NY, 1967.

——— and Hungda Chiu, *Criminal Justice in Post-Mao China: Analysis and Documents*, State University of New York Press, Albany, NY, 1985.

Linebarger, Paul, M. A., *The China of Chiang Kai-shek*, Norton, Boston, 1941, reprint, Greenwood Press, Westport, Conn., 1973.

Liu, Alan P.L., *How China is Ruled*, Englewood Cliffs, Prentice-Hall 1986.

MacFarquhar, Roderick, *The Origins of the Cultural Revolution*, vol. 1: *Contradictions among the People, 1956–1957*, Oxford University Press, 1974; vol. 2: *The Great Leap Forward, 1958–1960*, Oxford University Press, 1983.

———, *The Hundred Flowers Campaign and the Chinese Intellectuals*, Praeger, New York, 1960.

Michael, Franz, *China through the Ages: History of a Civilization*, Westview Press, Boulder, CO, 1986.

———, Carl Linden, Jan Prybyla, Jürgen Domes, *China and the Crisis of Marxism-Leninism*, Westview Press, Boulder, CO, 1990.

Moser, Steven W., *Broken Earth: The Rural Chinese*, Free Press, New York, 1983.

Mote, Frederick W., *Intellectual Foundations of China*, Alfred A. Knopf, New York, 1956.

Polo, Marco, *The Travels*, Penguin Books, Harmondsworth and New York, 1958.

Pye, Lucian W., *The Spirit of Chinese Politics*, The MIT Press, Cambridge, Mass., 1968.

—— *The Dynamics of Chinese Politics*, Oelgeschlager, Gunn and Hain, Cambridge, Mass., 1981.

Schiffrin, Harold Z., *Sun Yat-sen and the Origins of the Chinese Revolution*, University of California Press, Berkeley, 1968.

Sharman, Lyon, *Sun Yat-sen: His Life and Its Meaning*, John Day Co., New York, 1934.

Thornton, Richard C., *China: A Political History, 1917–1980*, Westview Press, Boulder, CO, 1982.

Walker, Richard L., *China Under Communism: The First Five Years*, Yale University Press, New Haven, 1955.

Watson, Burton, *Records of the Grand Historian of China*, Columbia University Press, New York, 1961.

——, *Ssu-ma Ch'ien, Grand Historian of China*, Columbia University Press, New York, 1958.

Weber, Max, *The Religion of China: Confucianism and Taoism*, trans. Hans H. Gerth, Free Press, Glencoe, IL., 1951.

Wittfogel, Karl-August, *Oriental Despotism: A Comparative Study of Total Power*, Yale University Press, New Haven, 1957.

Wright, Arthur (ed.), *The Confucian Persuasion*, Stanford University Press, 1960.

Wu Yüan-li, *Economic Reform in the PRC: Theory and Impact*, Hoover Institution Press, Stanford, 1988.

NAME INDEX

Publisher's note. The author uses Wade-Giles transliteration throughout the book. This index lists Pinyin alphabetically with Wade-Giles and Chinese equivalents.

SUBJECT INDEX

177